Praise for *The*

I've known Jenny as a professional colleague [illegible] than two decades and you can trust her advice, which she [illegible] intelligent research and deep thinking. Jenny also cares about her clients as people, not just about business owners.

You are going to find the templates, tools and processes in this book clear and easy to follow. They will save you a lot of time. Choose to read *The 7% Club*, and then engage with Jenny, and you'll be a long way down the road to fulfilling your goals and dreams.
Hunter Leonard, Founder Blue Frog Marketing and Silver & Wise, and ten-times bestselling author

Breaking through the $2M revenue ceiling is a challenge that most businesses will fail. Reaching $10M and beyond is rarer still… but it doesn't have to be that way. In *The 7% Club*, Jenny shares her hard-won insights and navigates you through the roadblocks to achieving these important milestones.
Allan Dib, Bestselling author of *The 1-Page Marketing Plan* and Founder of Successwise

Jenny has provided a treasure trove of gold throughout this brilliant resource for anyone looking to make their business one of the 7% of businesses that break through $2M in turnover. Her real, raw experiences, and those of others, are shared through powerful storytelling, case studies and brilliant metaphors and analogies. If you're looking for a guidebook that propels you on the path to business success, *The 7% Club* will accelerate your business and your life.
Renée Giarrusso, Founder, RG Dynamics and Limitless Leadership; keynote speaker, award-winning author, trainer and coach

I've built seven businesses that made it into The 7% Club and I've worked with hundreds more. The path to $1M+ revenue is highly predictable. Jenny has outlined the key principles for walking that path quickly. The frameworks and the ideas in this book could be the difference between a good business doing six-figure revenue and a great business doing seven- or eight-figure revenue. If you extrapolate that to the value of the business at exit, the ideas in the book could be life-changing.
Daniel Priestley, Author and entrepreneur

The 7% Club provides great insight into business life cycles and what strategies can be used to reach greater turnover but still hold onto profitability. Jenny outlines clear-cut approaches to multifaceted and complex issues facing CEOs and everyday business owners alike. Great read!
Sacha Caller, Founder, FliPro Pty Ltd

Where has this book been? *The 7% Club* is such a valuable resource for every business owner. Every chapter is stacked with valuable actions that will make a business better. This book will be earmarked, highlighted, underlined and written on in the margins as my go-to resource.
Ingrid Maynard, Founder and Managing Director, The Sales Dr

JENNY STILWELL

How to be one of the 7% of businesses
that make it beyond $2M in turnover

MAJOR
STREET

MAJOR STREET

First published in 2023 by Major Street Publishing Pty Ltd
info@majorstreet.com.au | +61 421 707 983 | majorstreet.com.au

NATIONAL LIBRARY OF AUSTRALIA

A catalogue record for this book is available from the National Library of Australia

Printed book ISBN: 978-1-922611-67-3
Ebook ISBN: 978-1-922611-68-0

Cover design by Typography Studio
Internal design by Production Works
Illustrations by Neale Jolly
Printed by IVE

10 9 8 7 6 5 4 3 2 1

Contents

Preface vii

PART I: Two Sides of the Peak 1

Chapter 1 My Story 3

Chapter 2 Let's Talk About Growth 7

Chapter 3 How Big is 'The 7% Club'? 21

Chapter 4 What Happens on the Path from $2M to $10M? 29

PART II: A Framework Provides Direction 43

Chapter 5 The Shift Business Growth Framework™ 45

Chapter 6 Simplify and Structure 65

Chapter 7 Develop and Lead 107

Chapter 8 Strategise and Scale 137

Chapter 9 Dealing with the Difficult Stuff 177

Conclusion: Making the Shift to 'The 7% Club' 197

Next Steps 205

Acknowledgements 207

About the Author 209

References 210

Index 211

Preface

If you have grown your business to between $1M and $2M, you have done an amazing job. It isn't easy and, although there is all sorts of advice available, applying it and reaching this level is a wonderful achievement.

If you have a business that is doing under $2M in sales and you want to grow to eight figures, there are key models, processes and tools you will need to use in your business to help you succeed. In the process, you will increase your own capabilities, skills and experience, which in turn will give you more confidence and certainty in growing a successful company.

Most business owners *choose* not to progress to this level and never make it past $2M in sales. There are various reasons for that, including their risk appetite for growth, the type of business involved, lifestyle factors and their level of drive.

However, I've written this book to explore and explain what is happening inside a business that *falters* as it approaches $2M. What are the challenges that stand in the way of the next stage of growth? How can they be broken through? Equipped with that information, we can map out a path forward that navigates these challenges and enables a business to grow past $2M to $10M and beyond.

In no way am I making any judgements whatsoever of those business owners who have gone from zero to below $2M. As I said before, it is an achievement to be proud of. The purpose of this book is to explain some of the factors that can inhibit growth from that point on, and why growing the next $2M or $10M can be a big challenge without the tools and models to help navigate this level of expansion.

One of my core philosophies is that the sole purpose of starting and building a business should be to enable you to have a better life in every sense. If your business has control over you, rather than the other way around, something needs to shift rather urgently. If you start to feel that your business is controlling you once you reach seven figures, resulting in you being overworked and overwhelmed, it's time for a shift. If you have aspirations to scale your business, you need to be the one at the controls.

My objective is to give you the knowledge and the strategies you need to overcome the challenges of business growth. I want to equip you for success.

In my quest to simplify complexity and reduce overwhelm, I've broken down the key challenges you will face in striving to grow your business beyond the $2M hurdle. The accompanying strategies will enable you to take control of your business and continue to grow, should that be your goal.

In the many businesses I have run, I have encountered these same barriers. Without the right advice and mentors along the way, it's so hard to know exactly what you have to do to get past obstacles and create better results without completely burning out!

My aim is for you to navigate past your challenges and build a better business – and enjoy a better life as a result.

I look forward to you joining 'The 7% Club'!

PART I

Two Sides of the Peak

AFTER MUCH RESEARCH and consideration, I have concluded that there are two types of business owners with turnovers below $2M.

First, there are those who start to climb to the $2M peak and decide it will be safer and more enjoyable back at base camp. They are happy not to proceed past $2M and to enjoy a very nice life well under that level.

Then there are those who head for the peak regardless, with every intent of getting there, but don't make it because the challenges are too great. They retreat, or they fail on the way up – or they don't give up and make many attempts until they finally reach the top.

Those at the peak have learned many lessons and scour the horizon for the next peak.

This book is for those who want to give it their best shot to reach the peak and beyond.

Success

Chapter 1

My Story

I started my first business in a recession – not ideal timing, but I disliked my job so much and the people who had taken over the company that I felt I had no option but to take my career into my own hands and start a business.

Prior to taking the plunge, I met with a recruiter I knew. Once he confirmed that there were no attractive positions available for me in the market at the time, I told him my plan. He advised me against it, saying that it was the worst time to start a business, the market was tough and I should wait until something came along.

The marketing consultancy

I didn't want to wait. I was excited about starting a business and 'being my own boss'. I was a General Manager of Sales and Marketing at the time, so I started a marketing consultancy. I had no reference points for being a business owner instead of an employee and I had no clients to take with me to open my business. Everything was from scratch.

In order to 'do the right thing', I called the recruiter a few weeks later to let him know I'd left the company and was officially out on my own – but I never got to speak to him. When I called the office, they told me he had left their company to start his own recruiting firm.

My lesson from this? Trust your capabilities and back yourself to achieve what you set your mind to!

So, off I went on my first venture and, although it was hard and slow to start with, it eventually gained momentum. I built a rather long list of clients in the IT sector (which had been my career background) and a growing portfolio of clients in other areas, including marketing, legal, textiles, cosmetics and finance.

About three years in, I started to build a team, which grew to two part-time consultants, a junior consultant who helped me on many client projects, a part-time office support person and several contractors for the more creative aspects of marketing that my clients needed.

I initiated a major research exercise, which gained me new clients but made little profit. I had too many people to pay. I felt like we were falling over each other in our small office space. Then, through no fault of my own, I lost a major client. My business was good until it wasn't. I cut back on all the people, did most of the client work myself and kept going. It was all too hard and unfulfilling. After year five, a client offered me a brilliant role and my marketing consultancy closed its doors.

Unfortunately, I never got out of the 'complexity' phase. I kept adding people as we acquired new projects and clients and, although the fees were healthy, the expenses eroded the profit. I didn't have any contingencies for the loss of a big client and the impact of that. I didn't have any advice and just did what I thought was the right thing. I see businesses going down this path all the time, and I want to tell them that they can course-correct and navigate around these early challenges.

CEO roles

After running my own businesses, I had several CEO roles running eight-figure companies owned by other people, including a publicly listed company. In these companies, efficiency was essential for profitability, processes had to be implemented in order to deliver in a consistent way and on time, and having my A-Team around me was crucial for me to do my role and be strategic.

I learned how absolutely critical it is to have a dashboard so your head of finance can't keep the critical figures from you. As the CEO, if something goes pear-shaped, you bear sole responsibility.

Communication, transparency and having a plan keeps everyone and everything in motion and helps prevent nasty surprises. If nasty surprises do occur, you have your A-Team to help you address them.

Through these and other experiences, I've learned the fundamentals of establishing and growing a business, creating a lifestyle company and dealing with the challenges of upscaling across 'Death Valley' (more about that later), and I've learned about many different business models and industry sectors through my clients.

There have been peaks and troughs, laughter and tears, sleepless nights and dreadfully difficult decisions. There have been casualties along the way and relationships that have endured for many years over shared experiences and perspectives.

The CEO advisory company

The next business I started was to provide advice, mentoring and strategic support to CEO founders of companies predominantly with turnover in the low seven figures. I helped many of them grow into eight figures.

This time I built my business on marketing and referrals. I grew my business with my clients by being very close to what my clients wanted and needed and helping them to be successful.

I helped them with some difficult decisions about people, customers and strategy, and to step back from running the day-to-day business to focus on growth and strategic expansion. In the process, they paid themselves more and significantly shifted their role from business owner to CEO.

Many of these shifts were difficult to make, but my clients persevered and managed to get through these barriers.

I learned that quality, not quantity, was key with my client portfolio. Working with the right client is good for your business and your soul! Creating intellectual property around what you know as an advisor is critical for differentiation, value-adding and being able to charge for value.

With both of my consultancy businesses, I navigated through the fundamentals of creating a startup, building a client base and a team, and becoming viable. However, with hindsight, I think I based these businesses on what I *could* do rather than what inspired me and gave me fulfilment. I think I was still finding my way with the right business for my future.

Now

I am excited to provide strategic advice and support to those business owners who want to build a better business, and learn how to navigate the big roadblocks and all the difficult stuff in between, to create a better life for themselves and the people they love. I am excited about writing books, creating intellectual property and being involved in my clients' journeys to establish healthy and successful companies that fund their lifestyles and become valuable assets to sell.

Two of my values are 'fun' and 'fulfilment' because whatever we do has to be fun and, in a business context, what we do has to add value for others and align with what has meaning for us, which leads to fulfilment.

So, it is in this context that I have written this book. It is these experiences and credentials I have earned, and these beliefs I hold, that stand behind my advice. With this book, I want to help you build a better business to achieve a better life and grow your company in a manageable way.

Chapter 2

Let's Talk About Growth

If you want to expand your capabilities to grow your company, we need to have a discussion about growth. Some people want to do grow quickly; others prefer manageable growth to a rollercoaster ride. Importantly, you need to know what you are going to grow and what outcomes you want from growth.

It's all up to you and what you want for your business and your life.

Advice is everywhere

When you're striving for growth, there is no shortage of advice out there to help you. You can get advice on digital marketing, content marketing, online business-building, scaling your business, finding investors, growing your team, thinking big, creating big goals, developing one-page plans, making acquisitions for immediate scale and making new products by attending seminars, joining programs, buying online courses, listening to podcasts…

It can be overwhelming. Literally.

The availability of extensive advice, instruction and information is truly one of the most wonderful benefits of living at this time in history. It's all there for all of us, in any medium. However, the flipside of this is that we can become overwhelmed by it. We try and absorb too much, and we struggle to differentiate the real from the overhyped. It can leave us uncertain about which way to go and what to focus on. We can't assimilate all the different pieces of information into a cohesive framework that makes sense.

When mapping out your company's growth, it's critical to have the right strategy at the right time, so you need to know what your overall growth objectives are.

What are you growing?

When I ask people what they are focused on growing in their business, most will say 'revenue', maybe followed by 'profit'. If the answer is only 'revenue', I usually ask, 'Why?', just to clarify.

There are numerous factors to focus on when growing in a company, such as sales, market share, geographic expansion, users, net profit, investors, capital, customers, valuation and share price. If your focus is on growing 'impact', you still need to be able to define what that means so you stay on track.

It may sound ridiculous but sometimes people don't quite know what they're trying to grow. I've had clients so intent on growing sales revenue that they've actually reduced their profit. Their whole focus has been on selling more and, in the drive to achieve that, they've reduced prices and ended up with plenty of customers but way less profit.

The more profitable a business is, the better its multiple will be when the time comes to sell, enabling the founders to be well rewarded 'on the way through' over the life of the business while they own it. For those founders focused on getting to a certain turnover figure to attract potential acquirers, the focus may be less on profit and more on investing in the resources that will get them to that critical turnover figure.

I've *never* had anyone tell me that they want to employ more people and increase their overheads! But big increases in sales usually result in increased numbers of people in your business. The point is, when you think about growth, you need to be clear what you want to grow and why, and what that will mean for your business.

Sometimes, what you're focusing on growing is not right for your business and has an opportunity cost, and some other opportunity would be a better option to focus on. For example, I once had a board director ask me what I was 'doing about Western Australia'. We were a national market leader with the majority of our business on the east coast of the country. There was a local competitor in WA who had the bulk of the relatively small market over there and a strong reputation as the leader in that market. They serviced smaller clients, as most large corporate and government organisations were based on the east coast. It was difficult for us to build relationships in Western Australia as we didn't have a presence there and it was relatively costly to service, and for the cost the returns would have been marginal. We could have considered acquiring that competitor but, again, the returns would not have justified the acquisition. The opportunity for growth did not exist in that market for our company.

So, my answer to the question was, 'We aren't going into that market'. Entering that geographic market would not have resulted in any growth at all. Pick what you focus on carefully as it will absorb your resources.

While this book is talking about growing sales revenue, specifically to beyond $2M, we can't just focus on sales. It's not uncommon for business owners to focus on sales to the exclusion of other variables, such as margin. I always say that margin is far more important to focus on.

If you win a major sale and are beaten down on margin, is it worth making $800K in revenue if it only delivers $40K in margin? This is a 0.5% margin, which leaves minimal buffer for any other costs such as overhead expenses. Would this be the right kind of sale to focus on? Would you want more sales like this for your business, or would you rather focus on smaller sales and higher margins?

So, try to keep in mind *what* you want to grow in your business and *why* that is important, as the right focus will help you enter The 7% Club.

'Go harder' is not the answer

Alongside the overwhelm from too much information is the pressure to 'go harder' and 'think big', and have a huge goal for business growth. That is *not* the answer for many business owners:

1. If a consulting business with eight full-time-equivalent employees was doing $1.1M turnover, should it 'go harder' and push to achieve $2M in sales?
2. If a graphic design business with three employees was doing $900K turnover, should it 'go harder' and aim for $2M turnover?
3. If a product-based business was doing $1.5M in sales, would it be the right strategy to 'go harder' and expand beyond $2M?
4. If a consultant working on their own was doing $500K in sales with minimal overheads and a few contractors for ad hoc support, would it be a good strategy to 'go harder' and aim for $2M in sales?

In all these examples, the answer is not, 'Go harder', but rather, 'It depends'. These are all actual examples and here is the course that each business owner took:

1. This client was driven to reach $1M in sales, which they achieved, and then they reset their goal to $2M. This goal was not the problem, but the approach was seriously flawed. In their quest for new business, they neglected existing clients and consequently lost their biggest clients. On top of that, they reduced their prices and, as a result, were winning smaller clients and needed more of them. To double their business required considerably more effort than they had resources for. The consultants in this company

were desperate for new resources to service existing clients as well as to go out and win even more new clients. They could have achieved $2M in sales and beyond with two additional consultants and some support (and winning back the big clients they had lost would have helped them get there more easily). However, the managing director refused to listen to my advice or the team's feedback and was intent on going hard to double sales with the same resources, which were stretched close to the limit, especially after a key consultant left and wasn't replaced. As a result, many priorities were left unaddressed because of lack of resources and focus, and the business was left floundering and unlikely to ever make their sales target.

2. This graphic design company could have continued to grow had they been more ambitious and had they wanted to. This was a classic example of owners who wanted a job more than to run a company and, as long as they ran their business profitably and looked after their clients, they were very happy to maintain their position, as it afforded them a good lifestyle. However, they eventually sold the business to a member of their team, who took it and flew because his vision was more ambitious. The founders got jobs with other companies and everyone lived happily ever after, so to speak.

3. The product business could have grown beyond $2M, but the owner steadfastly refused to step back and employ the right resources, attempting to grow with one full-time assistant and one part-time assistant. The constant daily demands were overwhelming. Eventually, the owner accepted an offer to buy the business because, in spite of all the effort made, it was in a holding pattern.

4. This solopreneur business was making mid six figures a year and delivering the business owner a wonderful lifestyle as a result. The lack of employees – just a handful of contractors to provide

support on demand – and very low overheads meant that most of the revenue was the owner's personal income. This business owner preferred lifestyle over investing in growth. Achieving $2M in turnover could certainly happen, but the owner would need to be clear on their own lifestyle goals as well as their business growth goals.

Again, it comes back to what you want to grow: Your own income? Your customer base? Your margin? What are your goals: To acquire other businesses? To sell one day? It's up to you and how you want to design your business model.

A startup in the cosmetics industry reported that it went from zero to $1M turnover in six months. It sold 200,000 units of its product. Therefore, by my calculations, those 200,000 units must have sold for around $5 per unit. If the production cost was $2 per unit, that would mean a production investment of $400K that someone would have had to fund upfront. Perhaps the contract manufacturer funded that. Maybe investors provided the seed capital. The founder of this business had a massive following on TikTok, which is where they launched the product. How would the business plan for continued growth based on escalating viral engagement? How quickly could the business be structured to support such growth? Where to from there?

Scaling up needs structure.

"Go harder" is not the answer!

There are many business owners in the cosmetics and skincare space with the objective to sell in their brand to a major retailer for a large first order. If they don't have the strategies in place to then promote their brand to generate the consumer demand that sells their brand through (which then leads to replenishment orders from the retailer), their brand and business is likely to flounder. Where to from there? What is the growth strategy that will enable them to regroup? These businesses pop up all the time, but they don't always become sustainable and successful.

However, not all business owners want to grow their business to $5M or $10M turnover in record time. There are boundless marketing and business messages geared around 'hacks' and 'scaling' implying that, if you don't grow your business fast, you're doing the wrong things. Not so.

Here are a few concepts that are worth considering as you grow your business. Some contribute to growth; others do not.

Growth versus scale

The terms 'growth' and 'scale' seem to be used interchangeably but there is a difference, particularly from an investor perspective.

'Growth' typically refers to incremental growth, whereby the resources required to create the growth need to be increased incrementally as the business grows. There is a logical correlation between the sales, direct expenses and indirect expenses or overheads required to generate growth. It can be planned and managed. It is how small businesses *typically* become bigger businesses. Even companies that grow exponentially through strategies such as franchising their business model still have a degree of correlation between their growth and the additional resources required to support and fuel that growth.

On the other hand, 'scale' refers to growing your business without the corresponding incremental increases in overheads – employees, space, equipment and so on. Truly 'scaling' a business at a rapid rate requires costly technology as the foundation, which usually requires capital from investors, who want to see fast results and rapid proof of the product or service concept.

For example, a software company needs resources to become established and to develop, test and release its software. Once done, it can add customers without needing a corresponding increase in resources as the customer base grows. Software can be paid for, subscribed to and downloaded by customers without costing the company anything extra to deliver.

Ideally, margins will increase as sales increase. The key ingredient is ensuring there is demand for the product and successful marketing to convert demand into sales.

Scale is growth on a faster and steeper trajectory. For example, Employment Hero is an employee management and HR system for small businesses; it is a software as a service (SaaS) product and has scaled quickly to have over 4500 users after six years of operation. New Zealand–based company Xero provides an online accounting system for small businesses and, after 12 years of operation, it gained over 600,000 users globally. Both of these examples were able to rapidly scale because of their technology platform.

Investors and technology startups aside, it is still common for the words 'growth' and 'scale' to be interchanged.

Enabling versus tethering

I wholeheartedly believe, and advocate passionately to anyone willing to listen, that your business must be a creation of your doing that will enable you to have the lifestyle you truly want. It is essential to not only create a business you enjoy but, more importantly, to build a business that actually encompasses your life goals and passions as well.

As I always say, better strategy leads to a better business, which will give you a better life. A business that isn't well structured or managed will keep you tied to it. That is not the purpose of building your own company.

The goal, as is the focus of this book, is to reach a level of growth that makes your business strong and viable ($2M-plus in sales) and you enjoy a good life as a result. That is the key.

I have a client who loves travel, and the thought of building a business that only has a domestic scope just isn't on the cards! Opportunities, contacts, projects – they must have a global focus.

Another client prefers to work alone. He's not antisocial and lacking in communication skills, he just doesn't want a team of people to manage! For him, a growing business with an expanding team of people needing mentoring and management does not enable the lifestyle he wants: it tethers him.

If you're an architect and you love to design buildings, you need to be able to do that. If you instead get caught up managing people and dealing with the day-to-day operations of a business, you will most likely start to resent being tethered by your business, and you will lose your momentum and your passion for what you do. If you recognise that doing architectural design is essential to you being passionate about what you do, then you must structure the day-to-day operations of your business to run without your hands-on involvement.

This is a real leap of faith for many business owners, but it is a true enabling step. Being able to design where and how you work is an essential part of enabling you to live how you really want to. Do you like to spend the day with clients, colleagues and members of your team, in meetings, out having lunch or in discussion? Or, would you rather be more solitary in how you work? Do you like to work at night or early in the morning?

Are the financial goals for your company driven by your own personal goals? For example, if you have the goal of doubling the business turnover next year, why do you want to do that and will it enable you to live more how you really want to? Set your business goals because they are in alignment with what you really want to do and enable you to live a great life. Don't set goals simply because you can and be tethered by them as a result.

Strategy versus guesswork

I had a memorable conversation with a business owner (not a client) at least 15 years ago who said they didn't like to have goals of any kind in their business because it 'limited' them. No goals, no clear focus and no real progress. That person continues to work the same way and their business is still the same size.

All successful companies grow with a strategy. There are different ways of approaching strategy but the key point is that, as long as you work through some process, it will galvanise your thoughts about where you want to take your business.

The strategy answers the question, 'How?' Investors won't assist with any funding unless there is a clear strategy around what the founder (or founders) plans to do with the funds to make the company grow further.

It's not uncommon for a business to take off without a clear plan and grow to the $1M to $2M range. However, as complexity kicks in, it becomes very difficult for the business to keep growing and be profitable without clear goals and a strategy for how they will be achieved.

I have clients come to me when they start to lose momentum and need some clear direction on the best way to move forward. They've reached a level of complexity that demands a strategy and a plan, or they've lost a major client and need to regroup and rebuild. Once your business nears the $2M mark, guesswork just will not get you the growth you aspire to.

For example, I started working with one client when his business was doing almost $2M turnover. He knew he had to shift from guesswork to strategy if his business was going to start making the impact that he envisioned. Once he had the strategic plan in place and the right structure in his business, growth took off. After 18 months his revenue had increased by over 150% to $5M a year.

It's all about taking your business more seriously and recognising when it is too big to grow any more in an ad hoc way based on guesswork and gut feeling.

The 80/20 snapshot

The Pareto principle, or the 80/20 rule, is a great analysis tool for drilling down into how your business is operating. In a nutshell, 20% of input generates 80% of output. The ratio may not be exactly that but it's usually in that ballpark. This universal rule is often overlooked by business owners but it is so powerful. It shows you which are the most valuable assets in your business and, therefore, what to focus on.

In general, your top 20% most valuable customers will create around 80% of your revenue, your top 20% of products will contribute around 80% of your sales revenue or operating margin (depending on which criteria you are analysing) and your top 20% of sales channels will generate around 80% of your sales. Products, customers, people, projects, processes, suppliers, expenses – most things in a business can be assessed this way, but customers, products and sales channels are the most insightful metrics for small businesses to analyse using this tool to provide a snapshot of what is generating the best returns for the business.

When I do a business review for a client, it is not uncommon for me to discover that they have hundreds of customers with only 10% to 20% generating the bulk of their revenue. This happens because of several factors, but a significant factor is the lack of parameters the salespeople receive about the type of customers they are ideally acquiring. Without these parameters, most of the customers the salespeople acquire will be 'low value'. If an 80/20 snapshot is never taken, it is difficult to know just how well new-customer-acquisition strategies are working and whether the customers being acquired are right for the business. (Another factor is when the company's driving focus is revenue growth and new business, which often comes at the cost of margin and longevity. Quantity over quality doesn't necessarily equate to profit.)

As your business grows, the 80/20 snapshot should reinforce that your goal should be to focus on and grow more of these types of clients and products or services. Focusing on the wrong things will result in negative returns.

Here is a practical example of this in terms of strategy: a client of mine produced products for the pet market and their 80/20 snapshot showed that 67% of their revenue came from 16% of their customers (see table 2.1). This is obviously not exactly 80/20, but it is indicative of that general pattern and shows the clients they needed to focus on.

Table 2.1: 80/20 snapshot of pet product sales

Value tier	Quantity	% of qty	Revenue value	% of value
$2K+	164	16%	$941,977	67.5%
$1K to <$2K	177	17%	$258,540	18.5%
<$1K	688	67%	$194,394	14%
TOTAL	**1029**	**100%**	**$1,394,911**	**100%**

However, what is interesting is how the business was *organised* to deliver these sales results. The team of mostly inexperienced salespeople was responsible for acquiring new business and maintaining (and growing, where possible) existing customers. They split account management of all these customers evenly across the team. This meant that a lot of resources were dedicated to servicing the 84% of customers who only generated 33% of their sales revenue. If the company were to do an analysis of the margin contribution by this group of stockists, they would probably find that it cost them to service this group.

We decided to look at other options for how that 84% of customers could be managed. We gave responsibility for servicing this group to the customer service team. This freed up the sales team to focus on acquiring and growing the highest value and less numerous customers in their portfolio.

I know there are people who would argue this point and try to justify retention of *all* customers but, when you know the true cost of servicing all your customers, sometimes the maths just doesn't make it viable. Focus your resources on where you will get the best return.

Focus first

The expression 'Ready, fire, aim' represents the antithesis of what a good leader does when confronting challenges of growth. Focus must precede action so everyone has clarity and is galvanised around a specific vision, goal or activity.

The overarching role of CEOs is to think first, gather information, reflect on their business, analyse results, make strategic decisions and keep guiding the business in the right direction. This thinking precedes action. Action and implementation then get the results.

If you, as the CEO of your own business, are not thinking about what is happening within and outside your company, and about your own impact and role in the business, then you may be trapped in operational day-to-day mode. If this is where you find yourself, you need to get out of that mode in order to grow your business further. Some of the stories already covered show unfocused CEOs who value action over thinking and analysis, and who may be focused on one thing to the detriment of others without even realising it. They are too busy 'doing' and 'going harder' to consider what's really going on in their business.

This book is designed to give you the framework to grow a sustainable business without you having to be in the thick of activity and implementation every day.

Chapter 3

How Big is 'The 7% Club'?

There is no ceiling to growth but we all know the statistics around small business failures in the first few years of operation. The reasons for failure are varied and are not the focus of this book. Rather, I want to explore the strategies that enable companies to break through the challenges that sideline the large numbers of small businesses that don't make it.

Unless the owner is growth-averse, or there is no market (or a very limited market) for the products or services being sold, or other factors such as a pandemic or natural disaster have an impact, or there are factors that reduce the relevance of the business to the market, there should not *technically* be a ceiling on growth.

But statistics show us a different story.

When companies start to grow, it can be both exciting and a little scary. The big orders and sales come in and celebrations follow. New clients come on board. Then comes the realisation that there will be a whole lot of work and change required for the business to fulfil this growth. It may occur quickly or only eventuate after a few years in business, but the impact is the same: business dynamics change, resources become stretched and new challenges arise constantly. Pressure builds.

In these circumstances, sadly, so many small businesses fail to continue their growth trajectory.

I say 'sadly' because it takes an enormous amount of effort, dedication, resourcefulness, energy, belief and persistence to get that far in the first place. To then realise that you may not have what is needed to push through to the next stage of growth can be devastating for exhausted entrepreneurs.

When do small businesses stop growing?

Based on Australian business statistics, which are quite startling (and all slightly different depending on the source but showing approximately the same indicators), it appears that **93% of all Australian businesses fail to break through $2M in sales turnover**.

I couldn't quite believe these numbers when I first saw them – 7% is a small percentage of businesses to reach $2M turnover.

It is important to note when viewing these figures that a large proportion of these entities will never have more than two or three employees *by design*. A big percentage of small businesses never want to grow big enough to necessitate employing a team of people. Some founders are happy to make enough to match the salary they earned previously working for someone else and, in many cases, this is the point when they elect to maintain their small size.

However, a large number of those 2,209,614 businesses doing less than $2M in sales in the Australian market are working hard to break through the $2M mark.

The following figures and tables compare Australian, UK and US markets.

Australia

Figure 3.1 shows the total businesses in the market. The light segment represents those doing less than $2M per annum in sales turnover and the dark segment represents those making more than $2M.

Figure 3.1: Only 7% of all businesses in Australia make more than AU$2M turnover

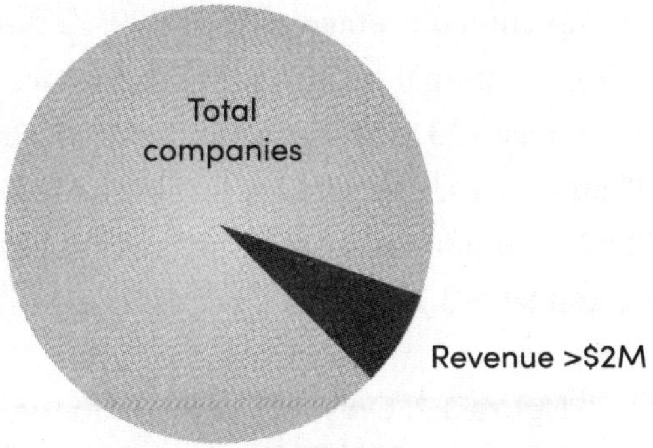

SOURCE: AUSTRALIAN SMALL BUSINESS & FAMILY ENTERPRISE OMBUDSMAN, 'SMALL BUSINESS COUNTS DECEMBER 2020'

When you see the actual numbers, it is surprising how many businesses make less than $50K a year in revenue and how few make over $2M (see table 3.1).

Table 3.1: Revenue brackets for Australian businesses

Revenue range	No. of businesses	% of businesses
$0 to <$50K	592,896	25%
$50K to <$200K	810,470	34.1%
$200K to <$2M	806,248	33.9%
$2M to <$5M	95,032	4%
$5M to <$10M	33,643	1.4%
$10M+	37,464	1.6%
TOTAL	**2,375,753**	**100%**

I doubted these figures when I saw them, so to investigate further I had a look at comparable figures from the UK and the USA.

United Kingdom

In the UK, only 4.1% of all small- and medium-sized businesses earn more than an annual average of £531,799. Zero-employee businesses average £70,000 annual turnover. Micro businesses, with nine people or fewer, average £531,799 turnover. Small businesses, with between 10 and 49 employees, average £3M turnover. Medium-sized businesses, with 50 to 249 employees, average just over £20M turnover a year (see figure 3.2 and table 3.2).

Figure 3.2: Only 4.1% of SMEs in the UK earn more than £531,799 average annual turnover

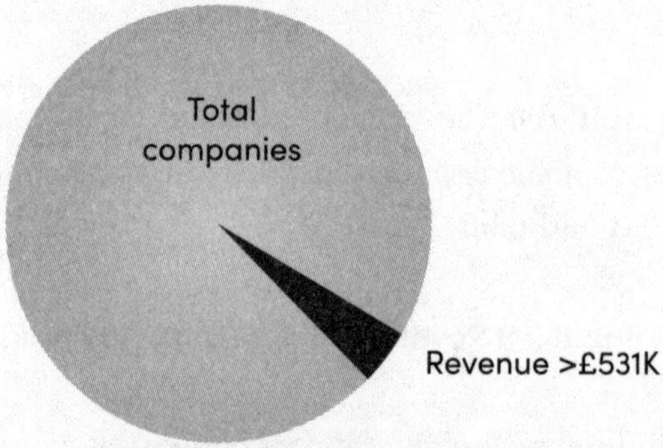

SOURCE: HOUSE OF COMMONS LIBRARY, BRIEFING PAPER # 06152 'BUSINESS STATISTICS' 22 JANUARY, 2021 BY MATTHEW WARD

Table 3.2: Revenue brackets for UK SMEs

No. of employees	No. of businesses	% of businesses	Average revenue
0	4,568,000	76.5%	£70,000
1–9	1,157,000	19.4%	£531,799
10–49	212,000	3.5%	£3,000,000
50–249	36,000	0.6%	£20,228,523
TOTAL	**5,973,000**	**100%**	

United States

Research into the US market shows similar results: of approximately 30.7 million small businesses, only 4.4% make more than US$1M turnover (see figure 3.3 and table 3.3).

Figure 3.3: Only 4.4% of small businesses in the USA make more than US$1M turnover

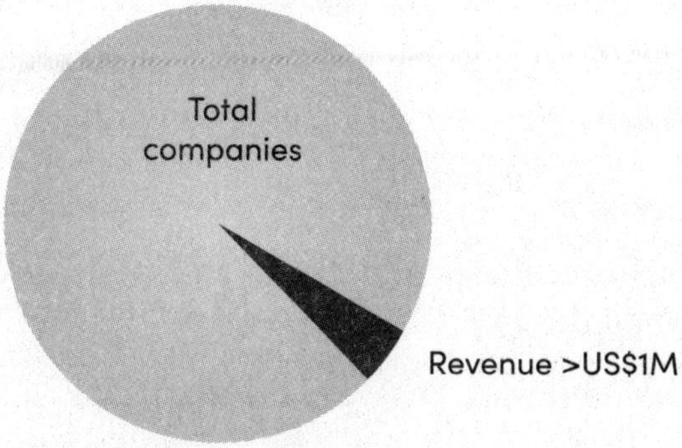

SOURCE: 2020 SMALL BUSINESS TRENDS LLC – DATA SOURCES INCLUDE THE US CENSUS AND SMALL BUSINESS ADMINISTRATION

Table 3.3: Revenue brackets for US businesses

Revenue range	No. of businesses	% of businesses
$0 to <$50K	24,813,048	80.7%
$50K to <$1M	4,581,985	14.9%
$1M to <$10M	1,230,008	4.0%
$10M+	122,992	0.4%
TOTAL	**30,748,033**	**100%**

Is this a universal pattern?

These statistics reinforce that this is not just an Australian market phenomenon.

These small businesses globally are run by women and men, by people under 50 and people over 50. Some are product-based businesses and others are service-based businesses. Some small businesses last a year, some grow with the founders and are sold or handed down to the next generation.

There is no apparent reason why so few grow to more than $2M turnover, but these are the most obvious business-owner motivations:

- They want an income, not to grow a company.
- Some of them are solo professionals who *prefer* the solo business model.
- They don't want to have to manage people.
- They don't want the risk of moving outside their comfort zone (that is, they know how to do 'the thing' they do, not how to have others doing it while they build a business).
- Some don't need to grow their business anywhere near $2M to have a profitable business that enables them to have a good lifestyle.
- Some don't want the risk associated with expansion and investment (and, yes, more people to manage).
- Some of the businesses under $2M are non-trading entities.

Growing companies face challenges around financing, people and culture, compliance, cashflow management, balancing growth with costs and making the right strategic decisions for the future. These challenges can seem insurmountable as you struggle to break through to the point where your business becomes more sustainable and manageable. Also, it is important to know that these challenges don't go away once you hit $2M in sales.

Companies can grow to eight or nine figures in revenue and, while sales are booming and product development is in overdrive, the business starts to outgrow the structure that worked so well when it was smaller. The supply chain for product development is costing more, promotions and special offers to win business at all costs are reducing margins and more people are employed to keep up with the workload. The management structure that used to be so well defined is now unclear and it's difficult to know who exactly is responsible – and accountable – for what. Sign-off and approval procedures have fallen by the wayside as everyone is so busy and there's no time for them. Communication lines become blurred and existing clients can be forgotten in favour of new client acquisition.

And then, one day, expenses are outstripping margin and cashflow starts to tighten. The company has become a little out of control, and customers and suppliers start to see that, too.

This scenario is not uncommon and has beached many businesses. That's why it is important to focus on *manageable* growth, with structure underpinning that. It is a cycle, and every growth phase needs a consolidation phase to follow in which the business can regroup and get ready to continue growing.

Maybe some of the businesses below $2M had a glimpse of this as they grew closer to $2M and decided they didn't want to go down that path, resolving to keep their size smaller and, for them, more manageable.

Barriers, struggles and Death Valley

The business management challenges that kick in as your company grows will test your mindset, resilience, risk appetite, determination and resolve for what you really want out of your business. There is a vast amount of content out there discussing this phenomenon and the fact that it is a universal pattern.

Jan Cavelle's book *Scale for Success* shares the view by Stephen Kelly, a renowned and highly successful British serial entrepreneur and tech startup advisor, that startups and growing companies need to cross what he refers to as 'Death Valley' before they can be considered successful. 'Death Valley' is the upscaling landscape between US$1M and US$10M, where so many businesses fall by the wayside or revert to being smaller (lifestyle) businesses.

In another example, Daniel Priestley, co-founder of business accelerator Dent Global and author of several books on entrepreneurship, describes the entrepreneur's journey as having several stages. He refers to the stage of growth between US$2M to US$10M as the 'Desert'.

In his 2002 book *Mastering the Rockefeller Habits*, Verne Harnish elaborates on the small business picture in the USA and, when compared with the 2020 figures, the picture has remained fairly consistent over the last two decades: 'There are roughly 23 million firms in the US, of which only 4% get above $1 million in revenue. Of those firms, only about 1 out of 10, or 0.4% of *all* companies, ever make it to $10 million in revenue'.

Each of these examples agree that companies in the upscaling zone from between US$1M and US$2M up to US$10M will either pare back and become lifestyle businesses, fail to make the journey or persevere and manage to cross Death Valley. Although these figures are in US dollars, they are also applicable in Australian dollars: the key point is that, at a point beyond AU$2M, a shift is required for a business to make it to eight figures.

The barriers and challenges that a company faces upscaling through this stage of the journey are discussed at length in this book, along with strategies to address them. As long as growth is approached in a manageable and strategic way, with a focus not just on sales but on all the important indicators, these challenges will be easier to manage.

The size of the business is less important than this concept: the challenges to growth will stop your company from expanding any further if you don't know how to address them.

Chapter 4

What Happens on the Path from $2M to $10M?

A $1M to $2M company is a very different organisation to a $10M company.

Reaching $1M is a very exciting achievement. The next exciting goal for most business owners is $2M and, after that, ambition is in full flight, with goals of reaching $5M or $10M.

A business can be grown to $1M with only a driven business owner focused on making sales, limited support resources and few overheads. At the beginning of this journey, the company's products and services are well received by a growing customer base. The first few employees are on board and the future looks exciting.

With continued growth towards $2M, the journey gets a little more challenging.

Do business owners run out of steam and enthusiasm on the way to $2M in revenue? Does it get harder to keep achieving growth with limited resources and infrastructure?

Possibly.

Do businesses grow to $1M on the back of one product or one service stream, and then the owner gets distracted by new opportunities and loses focus on the core business?

Possibly.

Does the need for more working capital and more consistent cash-flow place too much pressure on the owner and represent too much risk for them to keep pushing forward?

Possibly.

Whatever the reasons are, the journey definitely becomes more challenging as you approach $2M in revenue (see figure 4.1).

Figure 4.1: The challenging path from seven to eight figures

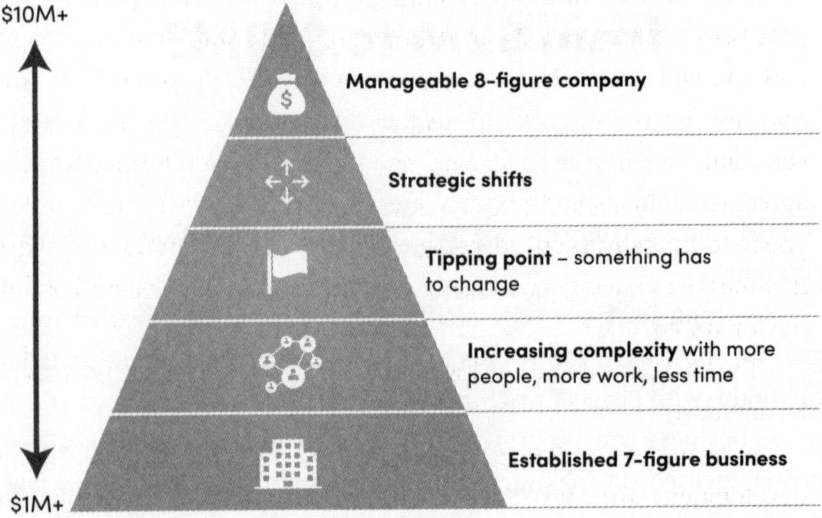

The <$2M business

Your business is a direct reflection of how you run it.

When you start your business, it is most likely that you are not thinking about future growth, business structure or even your own role. You are focused on winning new business, making sales, finding any resources you need to help you out and delivering whatever your product or service is.

As the owner of the business, you create your own ways of doing things and you are mostly the person who is 'doing the doing'.

You take on more work before you take on more people. You must stay in control because you are the only person who knows how everything is done. It annoys you intensely when someone doesn't do things exactly as you've shown them.

When you win the biggest customer or order you've ever had, you will have even more work to do because you don't have the right people to delegate to. You have no choice at this point but to be across everything because you can't afford any mistakes.

You may need a new system to track and manage stock more effectively, a proper accounts system and to implement new paperwork and processes as an expected part of doing business with your new client, and you will definitely need more resources to help you deliver. You may also need more cash to fund purchases of raw materials so you can fulfil your new orders. Legal and financial help is needed for new agreements, loans and possibly employment agreements and, unless you're technically knowledegable, you'll possibly be floundering when it comes to assessing, purchasing and implementing any new technology or systems.

The changes to your business are huge and you just can't control it all anymore.

In terms of the growth cycle of a business and the professional development curve for the owner, this is the most challenging stage of all in building a business.

Growth with products

As an example, a product-based company may have one brand with a handful of ranges that are sold into numerous independent retail stockists around the country. The brand may then have been picked up by a distributor and, as a result, has been sold into its first international retailer (usually thanks to some trade show success). There may also be an online store.

Selling their product range into a major retailer or grocery channel could suddenly add another several hundred thousand dollars to revenue, pushing company sales close to $2M.

So, right there in this example we have four different sales channels: online, international, independent retail stockists and major grocery. At this point, the business owner is usually focused on the following:

- 'We have to be online!' (Certainly, now more than ever this is critical, but it needs to be done well and involves its own level of investment and focus. It can't be an 'ad hoc' channel.)
- 'We can expand our international markets!' (This is even though the local market is far from optimised, and even though international channels have their own level of compliance, not to mention language differences, currency variations and other considerations!)
- 'We need to get into more stockists!' (This is even though there are often few specifics as to what the ideal stockists look like and which ones make the most sales and are the most profitable.)
- 'We can double our business going into grocery!' (Yes, you can, but do you know how this will impact your business model and operating margin?)

Sales agents may handle the stockists. Keeping the online store up to date may fall to the owner of the business, or maybe it is delegated to someone who can post updates on the store and social media and also look after orders. The owner of the company will be involved in managing overall sales – particularly the relationship with the grocery channel, the biggest single customer – and will definitely be closely involved in product development and production. This will be quite time-consuming as the production process has many moving parts and needs owner intervention and decision-making, purely because the owner of the business is the only one who is across *all* the detail at every point in the process. The grocery customer will have their own processes and systems that the business needs to align with; this can be arduous for the uninitiated.

After adding grocery to the customer mix, the business owner will need to manage that relationship at multiple levels and also continue to manage sales agents or major stockists directly. There will be more data entry and account reconciliation to be done, and warehousing and logistics is suddenly a bigger item on the agenda.

There will be bigger expense outlays for raw materials in order to produce a higher volume of product units, but national retailers don't pay as quickly as the business owner may be used to with other accounts. Now cashflow is becoming stretched. The business owner is doing more and more in their company and is excited about growth but feeling the pressure. They consider adding another 'assistant' to the team to help them cope.

However, they don't have good processes for employing new people, onboarding them and being clear about their roles and KPIs, and the owner has little time to communicate how things are done, where files are kept, and who key contacts are and how to find their details. The new people tend to flounder and be less productive than they could be for some time. The business owner feels even more pressure trying to bring new people on board and train them to do things the way they want them to be done. There is a lot going on!

Growing the business is exciting and they now have a glimpse into what could be possible if they brought another major customer on board. But, the business owner wonders quite rightly, *How do I do that? I'm already so busy, I feel like all I do is work! I could put another assistant on to help me. Would I need a full-time person?*

And so the conversation goes.

Growth with services

Service businesses have their own challenges, the greatest being the need for the owner to shift away from being the primary person who delivers the service to the person who creates, develops and enables a team to do the customer-facing delivery to a standard that will nurture and grow their client base into the future.

Growing a team of consultants, advisors, marketers, lawyers, designers and other experts requires a new approach to fee structures, understanding and implementing commercial arrangements, streamlining processes to underpin delivery, service consistency and quality, and understanding how to scale profitably while employing more people to service a growing client base.

The founder often struggles to step back from being the primary service provider to key clients. They can get bogged down in managing more people and more clients while still delivering service. For those with a lack of commercial experience, it can become more difficult to put in place the necessary structure for their business as they grow.

It is at this point that they are at their weakest and wonder how they are going to move past this point and become a well-oiled and successful service company.

The tipping point that makes growth unmanageable

What is happening at this point is that the business owner is so overloaded with managing the day-to-day that they can't lift their head up far enough to see what is *really* going on in their business and, importantly, they have little control over it. The business activity is controlling *them*.

What I have seen with all my clients at this stage of growth is that:

- they have limited numbers beyond the basic profit-and-loss figures, and they often get those way after the month has ended
- no-one understands all the core parts of business operations except the owner – most of this information is still in their head
- the business can't expand further in its current operational form or the business owner will break – the infrastructure to support growth isn't there
- the team is usually inexperienced relative to the owner, and they need direction and assistance
- the thought of putting more people on, who will need managing and who will increase expenses, is a barrier for the owner

- they have no time and little capacity to do any more than keep the day-to-day going.

They have no data because they don't know what they need. They have nothing to analyse or compare or drill down into. They cannot form any insights. They don't know what will help them grow past $2M and towards $10M, or even $5M. But they hope they get there.

Without any indicators to measure progress or highlight problems, the owner has no understanding of the dynamics in their business and where they need to focus. They don't know:

- which products or customers are really making them money
- which products or customers are costing them money
- the key ratios in their business
- the cost or contribution of their employees overall or by function
- if they could be more efficient with production
- how happy their customers really are
- if their suppliers are the right partners for now or for growth
- how they're tracking year on year except for sales figures and bottom line.

They don't think they should pay themselves too much as they might need that money to pay others. At some point they can become resentful because they see themselves as the hardest working person in the business and earning far less than they are worth.

Also, because they are so consumed with the day-to-day, they have no time to focus on:

- people – assembling, organising and aligning a capable team to help them grow
- strengthening relationships with key customers
- having sound commercial protection in place
- putting in place well-structured financial practices
- external opportunities, trends, ideas or relationships.

Without this understanding and focus, it will be almost impossible to grow beyond one or two million.

The $10M company

A $10M company, on the other hand, operates quite differently (although it has different challenges). The business owner has learned to run the company as the CEO and has people capability to take the day-to-day load.

This CEO has dashboards that show what is happening in the business on any given day, week, fortnight, month or quarter as need be. They can analyse what is going on in the business, compare it to previous periods and to the budget forecast and make corrections as required. They stay out of the day-to-day detail and instead focus first on the dashboard and then on feedback from customers and the team to tell the story.

The company runs because the team knows what needs to be done by whom and when. There are processes to follow. This gives the CEO time to focus outside the business as well and build key relationships and opportunities. There is an overarching operating system that everyone understands. There is data to measure, track and analyse business performance and 'need to know' indicators. There is a strong team in place and they all contribute. This company has no tolerance for non-performers.

The owner has shifted their role from 'doer' to 'leader' and is focused on growth and profit. They also have time for holidays, and family and friends, because they have structured their business that way. They encourage their team to do the same.

And, because the owner now understands what they are growing and how to make it work, they can pay themselves like the CEO they are. This increase in personal income enables them to have a better life.

What personal challenges face the business owner?

The impact of growth challenges isn't just within the company: they usually affect the founder in a way they have never experienced before, which in turn directly impacts business progress.

There are common fears like not being able to pay everyone when payroll is due, not being able to acquire any more customers or the dread of having to go back and work for someone else, or go back to corporate, if their venture doesn't succeed! They experience sleepless nights, anxious days and a mind that is always full of what they need to do and remember and follow up on and stress over.

Risk

Risk is a real concern as expansion is difficult without risking something. There are certain factors that can be predicted and planned for, but others are way less predictable and quantifiable. Once you've invested in new warehousing, for example, or recruited more (expensive) people, maybe had to obtain costly lines of credit or sign strict supply contracts with your largest customers, it's not easy to reverse out of those decisions if you change your mind.

What I've seen with clients and in other businesses is that business owners rarely do any risk assessment on what they are about to invest in for continued growth. There are no 'what-if' scenarios with worst-case situations and little realistic assessment of how big certain risks may be.

For example, you go after a competitive pitch to win a new client. Prices necessitate slim margins, contract terms are tight and service deliverables have high and measurable expectations. You go for it. But, what about the risk to your business if direct costs increase, or if supplier costs, casual labour rates, raw materials or exchange rate variations go against you? What would the impact be on cashflow and margin after weighing up these risks – both the likelihood of them happening and impact if they were to occur? Would you invest in a new building, or a new technology platform, without assessing the potential risk?

The risk of investing to upscale puts a lot of unnecessary pressure on the business owner if there hasn't been any assessment of financials and assumptions beforehand. Risk is a partner of upscaling – it is always there – but it can be too much for some business owners who prefer less risk for less growth.

As Richard Branson says, 'always assess the downside', and be prepared if it happens.

Overwhelm and frustration

You can't do more than focus on what needs to be done to service customers, manage your team, keep costs from exploding, fulfil sales orders and solve problems that arise day-to-day. You feel like you're drowning in everything that needs to be done and you never feel like you're getting ahead at all.

Overwhelm precludes creativity and certainly strategic thinking. It drains both physical and mental energy and keeps the business owner tethered to the day-to-day and just barely getting by. It is self-perpetuating because you have to keep going. Sometimes you want to stop and get off your own bus, but you have to keep driving it!

Once you're in this place, it's hard to shift out of it without help and advice.

Worry and fear

It starts to dawn on you that you don't really know how your business is going. You can see the bank account and you know there are still invoices to be raised for this month and payments to be collected. You think you're fine, but you have a nagging feeling that you may not be.

You know in your gut that you don't really have a grip on your business at all. You start to worry about this lack of control and fear that everything might fall over.

When big things happen – a legal or compliance obligation is neglected, a large supplier invoice comes in that kills cashflow (and almost kills you in the process) or a major client becomes potentially litigious because one of your team kept something from you (because they were fearful of the consequences) – they can create worry that consumes the business owner.

Lack of control, demands on your time all the time, not enough hours in the day, lack of sleep and flagging energy reserves all create far too much stress. When stress is a constant, it's sometimes hard to detect. Feeling this way becomes 'the norm'. The worst case is that your health suffers. That is *not* the purpose of creating your own business.

Overcoming these business and personal challenges is part of making the shifts that, once made, enable the founder to move forward stronger and wiser.

Doubt and uncertainty

When you start to second-guess yourself, because you're the only person around, doubt can become paralysing. You don't make strategic decisions because you aren't sure if they're the right ones. You want to grow your business but you need some certainty about the decisions you're making. How do you make the right decisions about the direction you're taking your business in, anyway?

That's the thing about growing your business for the first time: you are unlikely to have any reference points for important challenges and decisions when you need them. Doubt and uncertainty creep in. You ask others for their opinion, even though they aren't the right people to ask, and you fail to make any decisions with so much overwhelming input.

Uncertainty leads to lack of decisions and lack of progress.

It's no wonder that, with all this going on with the founder, the impact on the business will be considerable – and not in a positive way.

*

Anna's story was a textbook case of a business striving to make the $2M mark in sales but struggling to get there. She had grown her business into a viable entity in the first three years. She had a small team, all working part-time and very closely in an open space. Then they won a corporate client that would not only double their sales but change their business forever.

Anna needed help. The team was in overdrive but needed to constantly ask Anna for advice, help, direction and approval to do things. At the end of each day Anna felt like she had not achieved any of the pressing items on her own list. Instead, she felt like she was still the one doing it all.

She had employed one of her best friends to help out a couple of days a week. This grew to four days and her friend was doing way more than she ever expected. She was starting to flounder, too, as she only came on board to help out here and there on a casual basis. She didn't have a business background and was really struggling to keep up, feeling like she wasn't really being much help at all.

Anna was incredibly frustrated, thinking that her team weren't doing their job because they were always reliant upon her for answers and direction. As a result, she wasn't communicating with them very effectively because she felt they should just be getting on with it.

Having a new corporate client was something she had set as a big goal for the company and, now they had achieved that, she wondered if they could even deliver. Everything was in turmoil.

She was exhausted, unhappy and didn't want to be running a business anymore. She came to the conclusion that she just wasn't capable of running her own business, but she didn't want to work for someone else either.

Anna had no choice. She had to keep going, but she was overwhelmed and couldn't see anything clearly while she was buried in the detail of running her business day-to-day.

Her business had plenty of scope for growth well beyond $2M turnover but, without a new perspective, Anna was not going to be able to break through to that level.

Always the last out of the building, long after her team had gone home, she would drive home feeling numb but always a little anxious. They had made it through today, but what about tomorrow?

Eventually, another close friend of Anna's insisted that she call me for help.

This is a common scenario: a business reaches a particular stage of growth that propels it into increasing complexity, but it also increases the likelihood that the business will fall over itself and tempt the owner to walk away. It is critical at this stage that the business owner understands what is happening in their business and why they need to step up and run the company quite differently.

PART II

A Framework Provides Direction

I HAVE WORKED with many clients as a strategy advisor and business mentor, guiding them through the challenges that rise up to halt their growth. I went through the same challenges in my early career as CEO.

In *every* case, when something isn't working in your business and you aren't achieving real momentum with growth, *something must shift* in order for you to move forward.

Knowing what these barriers are, I have created a framework to help guide you when you need it: the Shift Business Growth Framework™.

There are three fundamental components that you will need to master in order to build a successful business, whatever size you would like it to be. The following chapters explain the framework and the components in detail, giving you direction and strategies to implement in your own business.

If you use this framework, it will help bring control, confidence and clarity to you as CEO and to your team as it grows with you.

Chapter 5

The Shift Business Growth Framework™

If you want to grow your business beyond low seven figures, you have to shift your focus. Figure 5.1 illustrates the shifts that need to be made in key areas of a business in order to upscale. There are three key obstacles that will impede growth and these may manifest at any point around $2M turnover.

Figure 5.1: Shift to break through and upscale

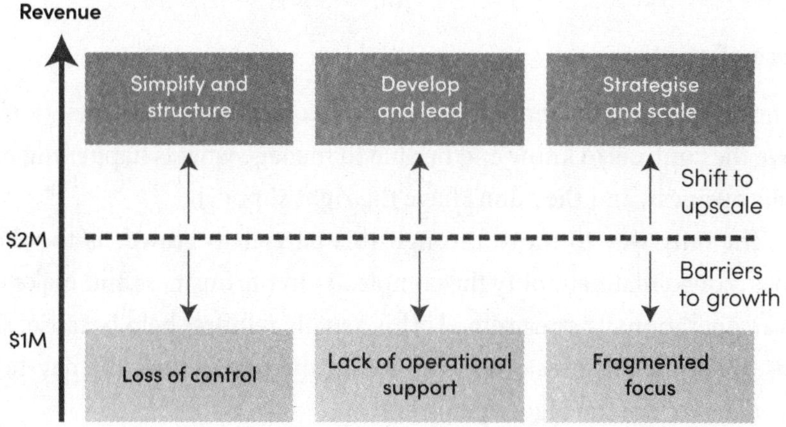

Throughout Part II, I share some invaluable lessons from those who have broken through the $2M mark and from some who have broken through eight figures.

Barriers to growth

As we have explored throughout this book, there are a few big challenges stopping companies from experiencing continued growth. They can be summarised by three barriers:

- **Loss of control:** when the business isn't structured in a way that allows the business owner to feel in control over what is happening
- **Lack of operational support:** the team is not fully accountable for supporting the business and the CEO, leaving pressure on the owner to help and manage a growing team
- **Fragmented focus:** the founder's focus is constantly changing rather than being clear on the company's strategic direction and priorities for growth.

Once the shifts have been made to allow you to break through these barriers, your business growth will expand at a far faster rate than previously and you will be headed toward membership of The 7% Club.

Loss of control

When a business owner is feeling out of control, it means they don't have the controls to know and be able to manage what is happening in their business, and they don't have the right support.

The only way to move through this barrier to growth is to take stock, consolidate, simplify the complexity in the business and make it more operationally streamlined. This usually requires help because, at this point, the business owner cannot lift their head from the day-to-day detail to see the bigger picture.

In the early days of growth, the owner of the business will be involved in every single part of stock production, management and distribution. At some point, this becomes untenable.

Likewise, as any business grows, complexity grows with it. There are more customers, more employees, more complex accounts and far more day-to-day business activity to be managed. At some point, this can seem like an insurmountable barrier to founders who don't know how to address this complexity, and they struggle to expand beyond their own limitations.

When the owner is out of control trying to run the business, this is usually exacerbated by the fact that they have little in the way of information or key indicators of how their business is performing. At best, they may know if sales are up or down and if they have any cash in the bank.

A business at this stage always has some employees, either full-time or part-time and on a permanent or casual basis. They have been employed to help the owner do an increasing array of tasks. This often doesn't work too well at this stage because:

- the owner is under pressure and has little time to provide any in-depth onboarding
- employees are given little direction in terms of how to do their role (where files are on the system, what processes they need to follow to get things done, and so on) because nothing has ever been documented – it's all in the owner's head
- not wanting to relinquish any control and not wanting to pay too much, the owner often employs people who could become good employees but who lack experience in what the role demands.

At this barrier point, having a team of people does not necessarily help the owner get any control in the business because these people have not been enabled to help.

It's like driving a car without a functioning dashboard: you're in the driver's seat; you have four passengers all asking questions and needing your advice, and you don't have time to help them because you have to drive the car; you think you have petrol in the tank but you can't remember when you last filled it; and there's a strange noise coming from the back somewhere but you don't know what it is. You're in hell and your passengers are not making the journey any easier! Would it be easier to run away and start again? You want to scream!

The burden of trying to manage all the increasing complexity is overwhelming. It's clear that you need to get your business under control as a matter of urgency.

Lack of operational support

This will be addressed more in chapter 7, but lack of operational support is essentially the lack of experienced resources in the business, preventing the owner from being able to step up and lead. Now is the time to make sure the right team, culture and structure is in place. A team that is capable of running the business day-to-day will enable you to step back and up to focus on your role as CEO and leader. Getting your A-Team in place will enable you to make the shift from 'doer' to 'leader'.

This step of becoming the leader is significant. I always use the analogy of the thirsty dog that doesn't want to let go of the bone in order to have a drink: the only way it will get what it needs is to let go of the bone. Taking the leap from operational manager to leader is necessary if you are to build a successful company.

In a way, making this leap is not dissimilar to the shift you needed to make when you first managed a team working in someone else's business or in corporate. Working on your own in marketing or accounts or sales is fine as you know what you have to do. It's all about you and your responsibilities. Taking the leap to then manage a team of people can be difficult. You don't know what they do, you don't quite know your role as their manager and you're not sure how to take the leap from managing yourself to managing a team. If you don't have a mentor to guide you, this can be a difficult learning curve.

You need to learn how to manage your company without being involved in every decision and action. You need to learn what a leader is responsible for. What does the job entail? It certainly will be very different from the role you had early on as the 'master doer'.

You have to let go. Letting go is all about trust. It is your job as leader to make sure you have the right key people in your business and that they are equipped to perform their own roles. You need to trust the processes you have in place, with checks and balances that will help you to trust that things will still work, and work well, without your constant intervention.

Upskilling is required to break through this barrier and make the leadership leap. The Shift Business Growth Framework™ will help you to break through this barrier. Once you have made the leap, you will be able to grow your business as a confident and capable leader.

Fragmented focus

Fragmented focus results in a lack of decisions or decisions that are constantly changing. If you don't have a clear vision and direction for your business, you will struggle to grow the right way. Without focus, you may grow in a haphazard way, not be as profitable as you want to be, end up in the wrong place serving a market you don't really want to be in, have way too many products or not enough services, or simply have a lot of resources being very busy without producing optimal results.

It isn't always easy to choose the right direction for your company or know how to make the right strategic decisions. However, unless you can move past this to take a more strategic and considered path to growth, you may not be able to upscale.

How can your focus be anything other than fragmented when you are being drawn to one thing after another each day, trying to have involvement in everything that happens in your business? Even if you were to have a strategic roadmap, you would struggle to follow it when dealing with complexity and an inexperienced team.

It is not uncommon to focus on the wrong things at this point. In my experience, many business owners are uncertain when it comes to strategy because they don't know how to approach it, they don't really understand what it means and, if they have a corporate background, they probably think it's a weighty and drawn-out process that has no place in their business! In that context there is usually limited analysis of their business to really understand how well it is performing, what needs changing and what the strategic priorities are.

When your mind is overwhelmed with the day-to-day, you do not have the capacity to take an objective look into your business and the market in which you operate. Without a clear focus and a plan for how to get there, and without the resources to support that drive forward, you will struggle to break out of your current situation.

In helping my clients grow, I work with them through all these barriers, and there is a massive difference between how they manage and grow their businesses before and after they break through these barriers.

For some of my clients, the pressure point is the people they have (or don't have) in their team and the unnecessary pressure being placed on the CEO as a result. They don't have the right people on board and it's causing problems. Decisions around people and structure need to be made in the context of financial performance and business efficiency. Looking at the gap in capability in the business often takes us back to a review of business operations to simplify and streamline complexity.

When a business is in growth mode, pushing through low seven figures, it is almost impossible to develop a strategy for upscaling without understanding how the company is performing with its operations, people and finance. Sometimes, a hot button initiates this process, and then the business is streamlined, strengthened and structured to upscale as a result.

As a result of these consistent challenges, I developed the Shift Business Growth Framework™ to provide my clients with a clear path and set of actions to reinvigorate growth and install control in their business.

The Shift Business Growth Framework™

The Shift Business Growth Framework™ outlines the three components for addressing the challenges of upscaling (see figure 5.2).

Figure 5.2: The Shift Business Growth Framework™

Simplify and structure	Develop and lead	Strategise and scale
Create structure and streamline operational processes for efficiencies	Attract and retain with the right culture both in person and remote	Confirm strategic foundations
Understand numbers and drivers of profitability Set up dashboards to run business	Build an A-Team to manage and take operational responsibility	Explore and assess opportunities using a framework to rate priorities
Map out key people and roles needed to support owner Reduce The Capability Gap™	Use The CEO Lens™ to refocus owner on value creation and leading the team	Get the team on board with a clear action plan and accountability for all

Simplify and structure

The whole purpose of this component is to bring structure to a growing business to make it more manageable for the business owner. Companies cannot go through periods of considerable growth without some consolidation, and the 'Simplify and structure' component delivers this.

As a business grows, efficiency, structure and knowing the numbers become incredibly important. Focusing on these areas will help the business owner make the shift from complexity to control. Structure and process become a critical foundation for effective business operations that deliver quality products and services to customers on time: streamlined, organised and efficient.

Rather than just running off a profit and loss (P&L) spreadsheet, more granular metrics are introduced that detail business performance and help drive decisions. People and business key performance indicators (KPIs) will be aligned so everyone is working toward the same outcomes.

Develop and lead

Once the right structure is in place, the business needs to start developing capability, with an A-Team of core managers to enable the CEO to step up and become the leader. People need to be employed for specific roles that fit with the resourcing requirements of an expanding business. They will be clear on their role, who they report to and what they are accountable for.

The focus needs to be on culture, ensuring the right people are in the right roles, and alignment of individual and company goals and KPIs. At this stage, the business owner will focus specifically on their role as CEO and trust their team to take care of daily operations.

Strategise and scale

Many business owners in the early stages of growth are unfamiliar with how to develop a strategic plan for their business. They don't know if or how they should involve their team in the process.

It takes quite a shift from keeping a plan in your head to making it real and declaring the strategic direction for all to follow. Making strategic decisions can be difficult without a framework and unseasoned CEOs often don't have reference points to help guide them along this new path.

It's almost impossible to upscale in a manageable and profitable way without a strategy. This stage provides a structured framework for the CEO and team to map out their business foundations, business insights and opportunities, strategic focus and game plan for the next 12 to 24 months. A high-level one-page summary gives everyone the focus they need to stay on track.

Overall, the Shift Business Growth Framework™ addresses these three key challenges that entrepreneurs need to take control of through their growth path while creating a valuable business. Once this framework has been implemented, the CEO will confidently take their business to the next level of growth as they have clarity, focus and excitement about the future.

The benefits of this framework are massive (see figure 5.3): confidence that comes from having strong foundations in place, clarity of focusing on the right strategic direction for the business, and the results that will follow. The best part is that growth is both manageable and profitable, enabling you to have not just a better business but a better life as a result.

Figure 5.3: The benefits of the Shift Business Growth Framework™

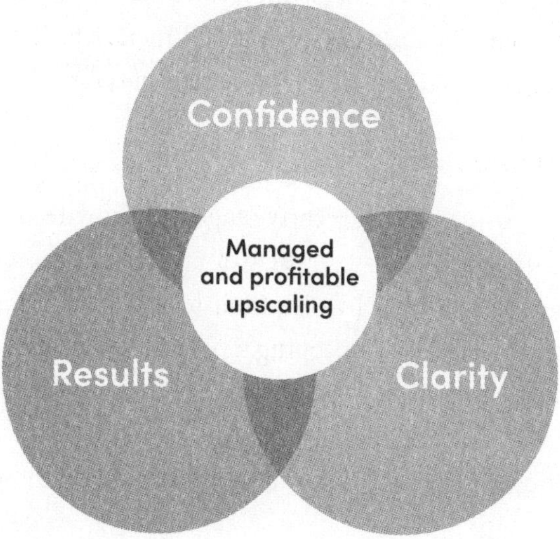

*

Each of the components in the Shift Business Growth Framework™ is explored in more detail in the following chapters, which are designed to enable you to jump in and out where you need to right now. If you are ready to make the shift toward growing your business in a manageable and profitable way, you can work through all three key components of the Shift Business Growth Framework™.

Breakthrough

Case Study: Think RAPT®

This intellectual property company is the creation of Renée Hasseldine. From our previous communication, through which we discovered that we went to the same university (several years apart!) and did the same degrees, I suspected Renée would be interesting to interview and I was right. Big on intellect and sense of humour, we chatted about all things business, growth and upscaling. Renée's book *Get Visual* (one of several she's written) is a great resource to delve into if you want a new approach to packaging and pitching your intellectual property (IP).

Think RAPT® started as a consultancy providing advice and support to companies wanting to identify and package their intellectual property to effectively convert more generic services into unique methodologies with compelling value propositions. Renée initially provided these services to her clients on a one-on-one basis – and we know that isn't scalable.

Uncomfortable with new business development

Renée shared with me that for 21 years she struggled with having to be someone she isn't. We're talking sales and marketing: going after new business, marketing to bring in leads and closing sales. She isn't alone, with large numbers of business owners knowing that sales and selling is both their Achilles heel and their path to freedom. So, how did Renée overcome that?

Let's go back to 2015, when she wrote her first book, *Share Your Passion: 7 Stages to Leverage Your Expertise and Make a Difference*, and had two or three large clients at a time. Renée said that once the book had been published, she took her business seriously.

Fast-forward to a short time later and Renée was attending a conference with her general manager. She was struck by a flash of her own IP and immediately dragged her GM (figuratively of course) into a café to brainstorm and create this new IP for her business.

The outcome of this brainstorming café session was the finessing and new iteration of Renée's core IP and signature program.

Her expertise was packaged into visual models to easily explain to her prospects and clients how she could help them overcome the challenges they were having selling their own services. Being able to easily see (via the visual models Renée used) how she could help transform their businesses if they worked with her made it a very easy sell. Suddenly, sales were easier than they had ever been, with workshops, and done-with-you and done-for-you services for one-on-one clients as well as groups.

The proof is in the pudding, as they say. (I don't know who says that but let's run with it!) Renée's 'Get Visual' signature system made selling and sales conversions easy and, in turn, brought a raft of clients who benefitted from the same transformations.

A new business model

Renée stopped doing one-on-one work not long after. She now has a different business model, which reflects a major turning point for Think RAPT®.

There are two key parts to the new business model: 'Certification & Licensing' and 'Craft Your Pitch'.

The future of the brand and the signature system is to continue to grow certification and licensing of the Think RAPT® system. Scaling-up opportunities are plentiful for Think RAPT®, and Renée's early restrictions with one-on-one sales calls and consulting are a distant memory. The business's new software platform enables the onboarding and training of new licensees. The company has four employees at time of writing and will be adding more as the certification model expands.

Drilling down further into aspects of the 'Get Visual' system, her business is focused on marketing the 'Craft Your Pitch' DIY model. It comes with some one-on-one consulting support from a licensee and future growth is focused on the US market because of its sheer size and potential.

This new model clearly takes Renée out of the picture as the key service provider and, with digital marketing helping to further drive leads to an automated sales conversion funnel, conversion is out of Renée's hands.

After heading up the business development role, which she has done extremely well for someone who struggles with 'being that person', Renée can now relinquish it and focus on her core zone of brilliance.

As Renée explained, with each of these transitions in her business, revenue has fallen and she has had to be the driver behind building it back up. Although she is less hands-on with sales and consulting, she now needs to manage a team, learn how to be the leader and take a strategic approach to how she structures the growth of the business. With a growing number of Think RAPT® Certified Specialists, Renée has been able to 'step back' from being the only consultant providing the Think RAPT® solution. She plans on being less hands-on running the day-to-day business, leaving that instead to her general manager. That will leave Renée free to be the leader, focus on the vision, drive strategy and embed a winning culture within her team. She can step back from the day-to-day but not from growing a company.

I asked Renée what the next steps were for Think RAPT® and her reply was 'eight figures and conquering the world'. She has a strategic plan and you can be sure it's all images!

Business lessons

- Get your IP right, productionise it and make it visual.
- Find someone to build your business with from the start – doing it on your own is hard and lonely.
- Don't force yourself to be someone you're not. Bring complementary skills into your team.
- Package your intellectual property in order to scale.

thinkrapt.com

Case Study: Tar Barrel

Matt Bebe is founder and Managing Director of Tar Barrel, a craft brewery and distillery on the Mornington Peninsula, south of Melbourne, Australia. Like Seachange Property and Green Olive Estate (featured later in this book), Tar Barrel takes advantage of the lifestyle focus in this part of the world, where vineyards are plentiful, craft brewers and distillers are thriving and the local community likes to look after its own.

I met with Matt in person and found him to be very hospitable and welcoming (of course!). He had requested our meeting happen later in the afternoon so he could 'have a beer' (naturally!).

Matt's story has an interesting twist: he sold the business after eight years, then bought part of it back one year later. But, first, let's go to the beginning of it all.

The backstory

Matt has been a local from a young age, so he is well-entrenched in this part of the world. Prior to starting his first venture, he had a career in sales training and learning and development, a perfect fit for his core sales skills and natural affinity with people.

Along with 20 shareholders, he started Mornington Peninsula Brewery because he had always wanted to have his own business. He enjoyed beer and breweries and had been in hospitality as a casual over the journey, so the idea was there to start a craft brewery. As Matt explains it, the idea took hold when Hawthorn won the AFL Grand Final in 2008 (not a date I remember, but let's continue…).

For the next year, Matt worked for around three hours each night on his business plan, with young children and a full-time job. He learned about the industry and about running a brewery and was fortunate to have an invaluable neighbour and shareholder as a sounding board. This was an important learning curve for Matt as he didn't want to waste anyone's investment in time or capital.

It took another six months to find a brewer (a critical prerequisite in the business plan) and a venue. Matt's role was to play to his strengths and take ownership of hospitality, sales and marketing, and finance. Being well-prepared and having a thorough plan, Matt was then able to secure $1 million in funding from 20 investors.

Given that running a brewery was completely new to Matt, some investors did take a leap of faith in backing him, and others invested because of the lifestyle aspect of being involved in such a business on the Mornington Peninsula. However, Matt is extremely genuine in his focus on customers and looking after people: important beliefs for any business.

From late 2009 to early 2010, they pulled the team and the new business together and took over a venue that was to become Mornington Peninsula Brewery.

Early days and growth

Growth has come from a strategic focus on local people and businesses. It's so hard to imagine but, when MPB started, there was only one other craft brewery on the Peninsula and fewer than 100 in Australia. MPB was well ahead of the curve.

Matt's approach to sales was to build relationships and always be thinking about how he could help people, knowing that sales would come. He approaches sales as a long-term game and not something to expect immediately. Relationships are key to everything he does in business and this has clearly paid off.

Rather than taking a blanket approach to selling, Matt considered who he would like to partner with and what sort of people he wanted to do business with. This included deciding which ten wineries he wanted MPB to be in, which bars in Melbourne selling craft beers he wanted MPB to be in and selectively thinking about other channels to focus on.

The brewery also won many beer awards, both local and international, and became known for being nice to deal with, supportive of the people it works with and making good beer (and the awards were testament to that fact).

It also became the first craft brewery from the Mornington Peninsula in mainland China. An executive MBA group assignment resulted in the group creating a full report and pitch document, complete with contacts, which was then given to Matt. One of those contacts, an Australian living in China, became the company's channel into China, taking 20-foot containers of kegs and cans for about the next three years.

Change of ownership and branding

Mornington Peninsula Brewery was sold to Tribe in 2018. As a result of a complex non-compete clause and the scale of the acquiring company, Matt was able to buy back the brewery facility 12 months later. The brewery changed its name to Tar Barrel. The next three years were a transitional period for the beer brand through the terms of the sale. From November 2022, the brewery and all beer and spirits are officially the Tar Barrel brand.

Matt has made the strategic decision for Tar Barrel to be Mornington Peninsula–centric. It is no longer in China. He wants to keep the brewery small and nimble and deliver what people would like.

Intentional business design – rewarding lifestyle

The team is lean, with 3 full-time people – including Andrew Gow, the head brewer who was previously with Matt at MPB – and 2 part-time, with 10 to 12 casuals depending on seasonal fluctuations.

This is a rewarding lifestyle business and Matt wants to keep it that way, with low overheads, high margins and strategic channels to keep the business both manageable and profitable. Matt works upwards from the channels in terms of the business model. He sees the key consideration being where you sell product, as that determines price points, margins and how you have to scale. For example, while a multi-store mass-market retailer of alcohol would provide a huge leap for the company in terms of distribution and revenue, the impact on the company would be the cost of scaling – people, equipment, overheads, lower margins and more complexity to manage.

This sort of channel opportunity is a huge lure for many businesses, but the cost of upscaling in this way needs to be factored in before decisions are made.

Tar Barrel received a new opportunity from a large local craft hotel and event venue. Matt had to weigh up the risks. His brewer had to increase his days from four to five, the company needed to bring in an assistant brewer and it needed to invest in two additional brewing tanks.

This opportunity was created, and won, because of Matt's investment in strong local relationships, and in getting to know and help out the venue's team over time before any business had been done. The opportunity was still a risk to the business. However, the potential exposure was mitigated in part by the ability to generate additional revenue from other sources from the investment in new equipment and people. The team is still lean and sales have grown as a result, with strong margins.

Matt has been selective in other channels, preferring to distribute in independent grocery chains (rather than the major mass-market supermarkets) and selected restaurants and hotels, as well as at the company's own craft brewery location. By having both small and large customers, and keeping them within the local community, upscaling is definitely manageable and profit is protected.

Matt invested further in the company's own offering, with craft gin and bourbon being added to its brewing portfolio in a few months. To complement this, he also invested in a smoker from the USA, so the company now offers patrons beer, bourbon and barbecue as well as the old favourite, pizzas. Expanding with new product offerings from its own location, which already has a loyal customer base, is a low-risk and high-margin strategy. Matt's three pillars of beer, bourbon and barbecue are now in place.

Tar Barrel's chef and brewer collaborate on interesting ideas for the menu, which shows they not only love what they do but are also fully supportive of the brand and vision they are helping to build.

Shifts

Matt's own role has been the biggest shift. He backs himself and, with experience, is now comfortable with his own decisions. As he says, he can see what he needs to do, he just needs to lean in and execute.

He has learned to let go and, as with all founders, that becomes easier when business activity and performance is measured in a dashboard with all the relevant figures and ratios for measuring and managing. Having an A-Team is critical to success and makes all the difference.

A constant is Matt's philosophy about doing the right things and getting it right: 'Be true to the beer and those who drink it'. This ethos combines his love for what Tar Barrel does with, even more importantly, the people it does it for.

Business lessons

- Understand the numbers.
- Have a goal and understand the levers in your business. You have to hold yourself accountable to deliver on those things.
- You have to understand how the pieces come together to create a whole business – it has to resonate with your customers.
- Stay true to your values and work incredibly hard. It won't happen without hard work.
- Don't rush. Understand what you are doing and why.
- Pay more for better, more experienced employees.
- The people in your team are like family – you need to look after them. Treat them well so they benefit from the business and enjoy the ride, too. Have a culture of looking after people.

- Values, family and lifestyle are important considerations for how you design your business.
- Spend money on what will produce the best return on investment.
- Know what you want and how far you want to scale.
- Where you sell product is the challenge to manage how you scale – small independent retailers versus national behemoths.
- Margins determine options – how profitable you are determines what else you can afford to do and invest in.
- Having a life and enjoying what you do is critical.
- Think big and act small – have people around you who you can discuss ideas with, read business books and keep learning. (I fully support that, too!)

tarbarrel.com.au

Chapter 6

Simplify and Structure

If you're serious about business expansion, structure is critical.

In order to keep it simple, streamlining and tightening up the following areas underpins a structural shift as you expand beyond low seven figures:

- profit
- process
- people
- dashboards.

It has been my experience that, in the early pursuit of growth, a focus on these aspects of structure is often neglected. Once in place, they will make a world of difference to how the business owner is able to manage the business without being involved in everything but at the same time feeling in control of what is going on. Feeling in control happens when you *actually* know how your business is performing because you have access to the right numbers, and you know there are core processes for your team to follow rather than you having to explain everything all of the time.

Profit

In order to graduate from the Australian Institute of Company Directors, there is a considerable section in the course content dedicated to understanding financials and being able to question and identify any potential anomalies or variances.

That is in order to become a director on the board of *someone else's* company. But, when it comes to their own companies, many founder-directors who don't have a finance background don't learn these important aspects of running *their own* company until after it has grown well into seven figures. Having this knowledge sooner in the growth journey will be far more useful as you look ahead at the strategic options for your company.

The purpose of this section is to give you some simple insights into the numbers and performance drivers that will help you to build value into your business and navigate a profitable path as it grows.

This is not a section on finance – I will leave that to the finance and accounting advisors. The purpose of this section on numbers is to provide you with some ideas for how you can put together a relevant dashboard for your own company that will give you greater understanding of how the business is performing and where attention may need to be directed to improve results. A dashboard gives you greater control of what is going on. It reduces the potential for any nasty surprises and, as the CEO, it helps you manage an expanding company with greater confidence.

I think it's worth stating here that industry benchmarks are *potentially* an indicator, but what's more important is how your business tracks against its own numbers. For example, there are different research reports that show revenue per employee figures for companies in different market segments (but they don't show profitability); I have had clients who outperform revenue per employee benchmark figures but who ask for my help because they aren't as profitable as they could be.

Everything outlined in this section will give you the data you need to start drilling down into your business and discovering ways to improve your own results. You can build on these and add your own ratios. Focus on your business results and not on what you think others might be doing.

Be all over the numbers!

The only way to be in control of what's happening in your business as it grows is to have regular updates on key numbers. The following subsections provide the fundamental numbers you need to know as a starting point and you can build from there.

It simply is not enough to have a profit and loss report prepared by your bookkeeper and provided to you well after the month has ended. If your business has grown into seven figures, you must be aware of the key drivers of performance. There are numbers for your business overall and numbers and ratios for different areas of your business, such as marketing, sales and operations.

Are your expenses tracking higher than forecast? What is the reason behind that increase? Is your projected headcount in line with forecast sales growth?

Here are some basics to start building your dashboard.

Profit and loss

Net profit, 'the bottom line', is the end-goal. Is your business making money? Is it a valuable asset? Net profit varies widely across companies and industries. It could vary from a loss to anywhere between 5 and 15% on average. Again, my view is that there is no benchmark – it is better to focus on shifting your own company's results upward.

It's important to see in your profit and loss report how you are tracking against the previous year (is revenue increasing or declining?), how you are tracking against the budget you have set for the month and year, and your actual result for the month and year to date.

This report can be in full detail, including a breakdown of all revenue categories, all direct expenses, margin, all overheads by item, and profit. I like to see percentages and dollar values for direct expenses, margin, overheads and profit. Dollar values might look acceptable but the percentages need to track. The relativities are important. For example, if revenue is increasing, margin needs to be increasing at the projected rate. If it has fallen, it means you are gaining sales at the cost of margin and, ultimately, profit.

Table 6.1 shows the absolute minimum report you should have as soon as the month has ended. The left-hand column can be broken out into detail or can be just a high-level summary.

In this example, the current month being reported on is April. Each month would ideally track the actual result for the same month last year, comparison to budget, actual for the month just reported on, and forecast figures for the following months to the end of the year. In this case, May and June would be the final months of the financial year for an Australian business. There would be a running annual total in the last column of your report for the full 12-month period covering the total for the previous year, budget for the full year and forecast total for the current year.

Table 6.1: Profit and loss report template

	Apr			May			Jun			Total		
	Last Year	Budget	Actual	Last Year	Budget	Forecast	Last Year	Budget	Forecast	Last Year	Budget	Forecast
Sales												
Direct Expenses $												
Direct Expenses %												
Margin $												
Margin %												
Overheads $												
Overheads %												
Profit $												
Profit %												

With this information you can track percentage changes year on year, which is useful as a high-level ratio. For example, if overheads as a percentage of sales are increasing, you need to drill down into the reason for that and address it as necessary. If sales look like they are going to be way under budget for the year, you want to address that as early as possible. If sales are way up, you don't want overheads to be up as well.

It is important to see this report as soon after month-end as possible so you can do what is required in the current month to address any sales or expense items.

Cashflow forecast

A cashflow forecast is essential to manage the survival and growth of your business. Without cash, a business will not survive. It is frequently referred to as the oxygen, fuel or lifeblood of a business.

I have known business owners to determine their cashflow position based on cash in the bank, along with a rough estimate of payments due in. This is a dangerous way to manage cashflow as it is incomplete at best and completely misleading at worst.

Your finance person can set this up for you. If you don't have one, ask your accountant or bookkeeper to do it as it is critical.

The sales revenue and expenses that are in the P&L all have timing variances in terms of when expense payments are due and when revenue is due to be paid to you. There will be other compliance considerations, such as superannuation, goods and services tax and pay-as-you-go tax, which will also have monthly, quarterly or annual timing.

If you have a corporate client whose terms are 60 days, you can schedule to receive the cash from that payment 60 days from the end of the month in which you invoiced them.

If you know a big quarterly payment is coming up, you may allocate a portion of that to put aside each month in advance so you have the cash when the invoice arrives. Make sure there isn't a huge gap in timing between when you need to pay your suppliers and when your customers pay you.

Lack of funds can be a barrier as a company grows and possibly overinvests in resources. More sales, better margins, lower costs, better terms – these are some of the factors impacting cashflow as long as you have access to the right numbers.

Update your cashflow forecast frequently so you are always across the flow of cash into and out of your company.

Margin analysis

I consider margin analysis to be an essential measure in any business.

There are businesses with cashflow problems because they aren't paying attention to margin. Not long before I wrote this book, I was made aware of a CEO running an eight-figure business telling his team to use a 1.5-times markup on their quotes. Their margin needs to be at least 40% just to break even; a markup of 1.5 equates to 33% margin. This company is going through cashflow problems because the team are using the wrong formula to calculate prices.

Something as fundamental as mistaking markup for margin will cause cashflow problems unless there are other streams of income that have pricing levels to compensate for low-margin business.

A margin analysis will tell you which *products* and *customers* are making the greatest contribution to your business. It will also identify where your products or customers may be costing your business. It will help you identify where to direct resources and focus.

You may have multiple streams of revenue from different products, services or brands. You may develop products in-house or sell someone else's products. Whatever your situation, it is not just about the sales revenue: the margin contribution these products make to your business is also important.

Some products deliver more to your business with less effort while others consume resources and add complexity to your business. Table 6.2 (overleaf) shows an example to highlight this.

Table 6.2: Margin contribution analysis by product example

	Product 1	Product 2	Product 3	Total
Sales revenue	$5,675,000	$4,750,000	$1,135,000	$11,560,000
Cost of goods sold	$2,270,000	$2,137,500	$703,700	$5,111,200
Margin $	$3,405,000	$2,612,500	$431,300	$6,448,800
Margin %	60%	55%	38%	55.8%
% of total margin	52.8%	40.5%	6.7%	
% of total sales	49.1%	41.1%	9.8%	

Product 1 is clearly the superstar, contributing $3.4M and 52.8% of the total operating margin and 49.1% of total sales. Product 2 is a strong performer with healthy margins and sales results.

On the other hand, the 'danger' is product 3: it contributes only 9.8% to sales and 6.7% to the company's overall margin.

This scenario can occur when, for example, the good performers are the company's own products, with higher margins, and the lower-margin products are third-party products. Alternatively, the poor performers could be new products in their initial few months that have yet to gain significant market traction. Decisions about which products to keep and which to divest need to be made in the larger context of all considerations.

Equally important is an analysis of margin contributed by the company's major *customers*. Table 6.3 shows an example to highlight this.

Most customer margin analysis would take the approach in the right-hand column of this table, considering the revenue from each customer (which could be consolidated over a year or be project-specific), the direct cost of goods sold and the resulting margin. In this case, a 70% margin would indicate that this is a highly profitable customer.

However, in the middle column, the real costs of servicing this customer have been factored in. There is a direct expense of $7800 for freight and there is an allocation of the account manager's time on an annual basis. (Let's just assume for this exercise the account manager costs the business $110,000 a year and they look after five major accounts; we could decide to apportion 20% of that person's cost to this major account.) Having added in these two direct costs associated with this customer, we can see that the real margin has reduced from 70% to 45%, and from $84,000 to $54,200.

Table 6.3: Margin contribution analysis by customer example

Revenue	$120,000	$120,000
Cost of goods sold (30%)	$36,000	$36,000
Freight	$7800	
Account management	$22,000	
Margin $	$54,200	$84,000
Margin %	45%	70%

As a business grows and acquires larger customers, annual reviews of the margin contribution for at least the major customers is a useful exercise. It is all about having control of the performance drivers in your business and being able to focus on whatever needs adjustment or attention.

It is not an entirely uncommon practice for businesses to neglect reviewing fees and pricing schedules, keeping customers on the same rates they have had for years. Meanwhile, real costs to service their customers are increasing, impacting margins and overall company profitability significantly.

Before we leave margins, I think it is important to mention sales and selling, particularly if the founder of the business is also the primary salesperson.

It can be very easy to say 'yes' to new business that is priced too low, especially if the main focus is revenue. It is not good business to win a pitch for several hundred thousand dollars or several million dollars if that provides for little margin because the pricing is way under what the company would normally charge. It is one way to increase revenue but it can also cause cashflow problems and, at the very least, reduce margins and profitability.

Revenue per employee

A business needs to produce a return on investment (ROI) from all the assets and resources employed by the company. This includes an ROI from the employees. If you have too many employees relative to your company's turnover, your costs are going to be higher than they need to be.

When a business is in growth mode and in the process of adding more people to the team, revenue is increasing but costs are typically growing at the same time. The goal is to find a balance between minimising costs, operating as efficiently as you can (good people, good systems and processes, good reporting on key performance indicators) and having the right number of people employed for the current level of business you're doing.

Revenue per employee and profit per employee are good indicators to use. They tell you how many people you are using to get the results you are getting. Your headcount will rise to both drive and support your sales revenue, but it needs to be relative.

If revenue per employee is declining year on year as your turnover grows, it means you're being less efficient in your use of resources. It often means you haven't streamlined your procedures and put better systems in place to support growth.

Business owners often 'throw people' at problems rather than solve the problems and make the business run more efficiently first. This combination of not having good systems and adding more and more people to help manage your business is a recipe for increasing complexity and costs.

Revenue per employee provides a quick reference of how efficiently the business is utilising resources relative to revenue. This ratio is worth checking on an annual basis, or more frequently if expansion is occurring rapidly.

When comparing one year to another, as in table 6.4, increasing revenue per employee ratios can be indicative of the business operating more efficiently, or it could demonstrate that employees are being pushed to their limits and need support from additional team members.

To calculate revenue per employee, divide total revenue over a 12-month period by the number of full-time employees in the company.

Table 6.4: Year on year revenue comparison example

	Revenue 3 years ago	Revenue 2 years ago	Revenue last year	Projected revenue this year
Total revenue	$6,100,000	$7,500,000	$10,000,000	$12,000,000
No. of employees	16	19	17	17
Revenue per employee	$381,250	$394,737	$588,235	$705,882
Net profit $	$550,000	$600,000	$1,000,000	$1,200,000
Net profit %	9%	8%	10%	10%
Net profit per employee	$34,375	$31,579	$58,823	$70,588

What this example shows is that revenue per employee is climbing. Sales have virtually doubled with approximately the same number of people over the three years. Profit has grown overall and per employee, which would indicate that the company is doing things far more efficiently with the same number of people.

It *could* also indicate that the current team is close to its limit and another one or two people could be brought on board. The only way for you to fully assess that is to talk to your team and get their feedback (and assess their performance and stress levels) and evaluate how smoothly your operations are working.

Of course, every business has revenue-generating employees and those who are in support roles. This ratio is also interesting to look at as a business grows because, if the business is becoming heavier with support people, this could indicate inefficient processes that need more people, the sales-generating resources need to raise their output, or some other issue, such as the need for price reviews.

Calculating the revenue per employee ratio could raise some questions that need answering:

- Is the business about as complex or a lot more complex than it was a few years ago?
- Do the overall operations run smoothly or with more and more glitches?
- Do I need to increase or reduce the number of employees?
- Do we need to improve our systems and efficiencies?

Projected revenue and headcount

Projected revenue and headcount is a useful metric when planning for growth and additional resources. This ratio looks *ahead*, rather than backward as the previous ratio does.

In the example in table 6.5, it is clear that *planned* growth in headcount is in line with projected revenue growth. Revenue per employee is healthy and growing, although it is likely that an additional resource may be needed this year given the significant growth path projected over the previous two years.

However, it is also clear that, as the business grows and revenue increases, the ratio of support staff to revenue-generating people is growing. This needs monitoring. Two years ago, 2 of the 8 team members (25%) were in sales. The projected ratio this year falls to 20% (3 of 15).

This is a very simple tool for a growing business to use as it puts resources, revenue and returns on investing in additional resources into perspective in the one table. Simple but effective.

Table 6.5: Projected revenue and headcount example

	Two years ago	Last year	This year
MD's office	1	1	2
Finance/admin	1	2	2
Sales/account management	2	3	3
Tech support	2	3	4
Project managers/developers	2	3	4
TOTAL EMPLOYEES	8	12	15
Forecast revenue	$2,000,000	$3,500,000	$5,500,000
Revenue per employee	$250,000	$291,667	$366,667

Some other people indicators

Other people indicators that may be relevant to your business include:

- employee turnover
- employee feedback scores
- training costs
- absenteeism
- long-service-leave accruals.

Again, which ones are relevant to you will depend on your business model.

Marketing indicators

To measure the effectiveness (outcomes) of marketing spend, start with where you are investing money in marketing. Some easy indicators include:

- new leads – for example, from a specific marketing activity or promotion
- cost per lead
- campaign sales revenue value
- conversions as a percentage of leads
- cost per new client acquisition
- numbers of attendees per event
- leads generated per event
- clients acquired / conversion from event leads
- new subscribers
- email open rates
- number of new followers
- number of referrals
- number of new clients per month/quarter/year
- average transaction value
- transaction frequency
- breakdown of existing clients by value – for example, five Tier 1 clients (compared with two in the previous year)
- retainer versus non-retainer clients
- ratio of new clients acquired per year relative to existing clients
- net promoter score.

It is important to remember that any ratios or indicators must be relevant to your business and your marketing activities. If number of new followers makes you feel good but doesn't equate to sales, then use more relevant indicators to measure your company's marketing performance.

Operational indicators

Again, the important indicators will be those that show whether and how well you have delivered to your customers. Service and product companies will differ significantly, and which indicators you choose will need to add insights about how your business operates. Some questions to ask might include the following:

- Was the product acceptable or were there defects?
- How many calls were handled by your technical support team?
- Were they all solved and closed off?
- Were all delivery schedule dates met on time?
- How many replenishment orders have been received – by quantity and by value?

The key answers you need are whether you delivered in full and on time without any issues, defects or delays. The cost of delays and defects is essential. Employee churn rates are important for labour-intensive businesses. Production rates and daily volumes show operating efficiency.

In order to simplify the important measures, look at what you are delivering to customers, how it is delivered and the resources required. Then, put some measures around this for your own business.

KPIs and other indicators of business performance need to be simple, measurable and relevant to your company. Don't over-engineer it. Measures around financial performance are critical, as are measures around people. Tracking marketing and sales results is critical for growth, and operational measures track how well the business delivers products and services to your customers.

Keep it as simple and meaningful as possible. Remember, you just need indicators that will help you upscale your business in a manageable and profitable way.

Process

Just for a moment, let's draw an unusual comparison between the activities in your business and unloading a dishwasher.

In this example, there are two different people doing this exercise. They are both allowed to call for backup. Overworked Ollie goes first.

The facilitator asks Ollie to unload the contents of the dishwasher. Ollie doesn't know where the cupboards and storage places are to put the clean items into and he has no idea what is in the dishwasher. The facilitator gives him one minute to complete the task from the time he removes the first item.

Ollie opens the dishwasher and the timer starts. He immediately starts removing clean plates and glasses. He piles them all up on the kitchen benchtops, and the piles get bigger and bigger. Ollie is definitely getting a bit frazzled. He tries to go faster but then he drops a glass! *What am I meant to do now?* he wonders in a panic. He starts frantically pulling open a few cupboards and drawers, but they don't seem to be the right places for plates and glasses. The clock is ticking. With 40 seconds gone, he requests someone to help.

The helper comes in. Ollie expects them to unload and put dishes away. Unfortunately, the helper just stands there with a rather gormless look on his face and asks Ollie, 'What do you want me to do?' Ollie screams at him, 'Help me unload the dishwasher!' The helper just stands there and says, 'How?' This winds Ollie up even more and he can't concentrate on what he is meant to achieve. The timer goes off. Ollie is apoplectic and retreats to the corner seat, head pounding. He takes the glass of wine and two paracetamol that are offered by the facilitator.

Next up is Organised Olivia. She opens the dishwasher and assesses the extent of the unpacking that will be required. Then she opens all the drawers and cupboards in the kitchen and adjacent dining area and locates where the items from the dishwasher will need to be stored.

Overworked Ollie interjects, 'I wasn't allowed to do that!'

'Yes, you were,' says the facilitator. 'The timer doesn't start until you remove the first item from the dishwasher. You could have done exactly the same thing but you were too busy "doing" instead of listening and thinking.'

Organised Olivia starts. She methodically unpacks all the same items from the dishwasher and places them directly into their storage area: glasses first, then cups and mugs, then plates, then saucepans and baking dishes, and finally cutlery.

The timer goes off: 50 seconds and done. Olivia smiles and sits down.

Ollie is furious and on his second glass of wine. He wants to know how Olivia did it so easily and why he had so much trouble. He also demands to know why he had such a useless helper.

'Let me explain,' says the facilitator:

> First of all, you didn't *think* about what you had to do and you didn't *listen* to my instructions – you just wanted to take action and do it *fast*. By putting everything on the bench first, you wasted time *double-handling*, which is very inefficient.
>
> You asked for an assistant but *failed to instruct them* on what to do. You yelled and were rude, so the assistant was reluctant to help. It wasn't the assistant that was useless, it was your complete *lack of direction* and *poor leadership* that resulted in the unsatisfactory outcome.
>
> Olivia has just documented the process for you, along with the instructions for where things go, and has briefed the helper. Let's run through this one more time and see if you can do it in under a minute now. And, you can put down that glass of wine before you start – we don't want another broken glass!

The Gating Process™ is designed to transform your company's 'operating system' from Overworked Ollie to Organised Olivia. It is a tool I have developed to help my clients extract information from the business owner's head so the rest of the team can access it.

The person who starts a business designs or sets up how things are to work – how services are delivered to clients, how products are developed, how the online store operates once someone places an order and so on – for most key processes in the company. The trouble is, as the business grows, there is only one person who knows how everything in the business is meant to work. As a result, the owner gets frustrated when the team isn't sure how to do things or does things incorrectly (or just differently), which further reinforces in the owner's mind that they need to do everything anyway!

At this point, the owner questions why they are adding more people to the team when they still have to step in and assist them all the time. The fact that they need to step in at some point creates a bottleneck, with the business owner being required to explain, teach and make checks at many points in the process. This bottleneck contributes to increasing complexity and a feeling of being constantly under pressure.

The Gating Process™ is simply a tool to map out every stage within each core process in the business so everyone can see what is meant to be done, by whom and at which points in the process. It brings clarity to confusion and streamlines what can potentially be complex processes.

The idea of the 'gating' is that each part of the process needs to be entered into a system, documented or completed in some way before it can proceed through the 'gate' to the next stage of the process. This is a way of implementing checks and balances so the team understands what needs to be done and how, and the business owner can be more confident that important functions in the business are being done the right way.

It isn't hard to do but it can take a while to map out a complex process with your team for the very first time. Here's how to document The Gating Process™:

1. Start with the very first step and keep asking questions like, 'What happens next?', 'Who does that?', 'Where is the data entered?', 'Who approves that step?', 'When does it need to be done?' and so on. Use sticky notes, write actions on them and then move them around if they end up being in the wrong positions.
2. Challenge how things are done currently by exploring whether they could be done faster and with fewer people involved at that point in the process, or whether that step could be removed or placed somewhere else.
3. Make sure you name your processes – for example, 'New Client Onboarding Process'. This will help everything make sense once you start mapping out the core processes in your own business.
4. When everyone has agreed on the process, document it and review it for updates and accuracy every six months.

Product development is a process. Service delivery is a process. Recruitment and onboarding is a key process. Also, certain departments or roles – such as finance, operations and marketing – will have their own core processes.

This is not about creating a detailed operations manual; it is just about clarifying and documenting the core processes so everyone can follow them.

There are many benefits of The Gating Process™ but, ultimately, the main benefit of more efficiently managed processes is that they enable your business to upscale in a more manageable and profitable way.

Here are some other benefits of The Gating Process™:

- It acts as the company DNA – it becomes part of the culture around 'the company way' and how your company does what it does.
- It helps the people in your business do their jobs.
- It helps free the business owner from being involved in every single step.
- It helps engender trust in the team by the founder because processes are more repeatable and reliable.
- It gives everyone confidence knowing that they understand and can follow key processes.
- It makes it so easy to bring new people into the business as it fast-tracks their learning curve.
- It saves time, reduces errors, unlocks bottlenecks and improves efficiency.
- Once in place, it helps map out resource requirements for the key things in your core processes that need to be done.

People

One of the key people challenges that occurs as a business upscales is bringing on board the right people at the right time.

I understand starting small and employing less experienced and less expensive people until the business has more funds available for investing in the right people. However, one experienced and capable person will always contribute more to the growth of your business than two less experienced people and will make progress faster. They will be less reliant on you.

Allowing the wrong people to stay in your business for too long is another challenge for most business owners, who avoid the difficult decisions and conversations around letting those people go.

At its most extreme, having too many people issues in your business will leave you drained, frustrated and even resentful because it seems that no-one in the business is taking responsibility for anything except you. Enduring these challenges on a daily basis takes you away from your own role, often deprives you of sleep, takes you away from family and friends and can leave you wondering if growth is really worth it. If you're going to move past these challenges, you really need to be prepared to be decisive and committed to making the changes required that will fully support you as the CEO.

More experience and more capability produces results faster.

The Capability Gap™

Building capability in your team will enable you to make the shift from 'doer' to 'leader'. This is a big step.

Standing in the way of this step is The Capability Gap™ (see figure 6.1). It causes a lot of problems in growing businesses and makes founders ill-equipped to grow capable teams. This gap in capability and experience between the business owner and the next most experienced person or people in a small but growing business is a problem. It is also a hurdle to overcome if you want to upscale with the right people in place.

Figure 6.1: The Capability Gap™

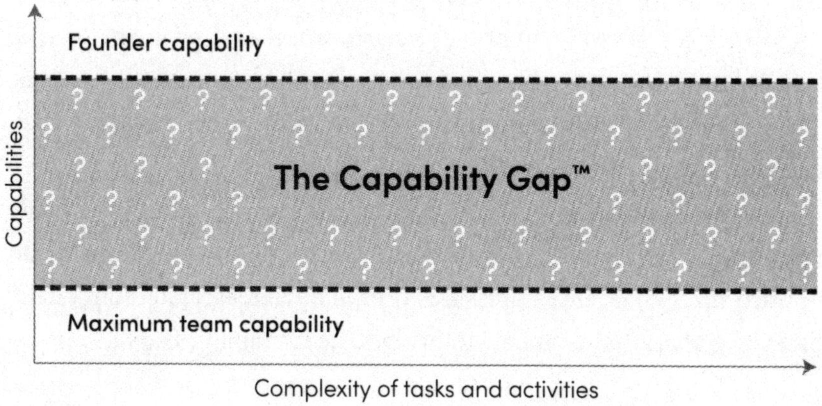

It does take a leap of faith to employ more experienced – and more expensive – people to join your team while being mindful of overheads as you upscale.

The Capability Gap™ is usually big. Avoiding employing the right (more experienced) people when the business and owner need it most is due to several factors, most of which are based in fear:

- The business owner lacks certainty around what resources or structure is needed, beyond some help with daily tasks, so they employ someone to do low-end tasks rather than taking on someone who would be capable of much more responsibility.
- They are reluctant to pay too much, especially if it means the new person is earning close to what the owner is paid.
- They hold back on making this investment into their business because they fear making this commitment.
- They are unsure how to work with or manage a more senior or experienced employee.
- Control issues are perpetuating a fear of letting go.

The inexperience gap results in questions and problems reverting back to the owner, who is the only person with enough experience to address certain situations. This doesn't actually help the owner or the business. It means the company's employees still need to go to the owner for answers, approvals, clarification and problem-solving because they don't have the capability to handle problems themselves. There are more people in the business, and more costs because of that, and the business owner is still mired in the day-to-day.

As the business grows and becomes more complex, with more tasks and activities to be completed, all questions and problems are an upward force that places pressures on the owner, escalated on a daily basis by a team that is unable to bridge The Capability Gap™.

It does take a leap of faith to close The Capability Gap™, and the leap is essential to upscaling. So, how do you move closer to taking this leap?

In my experience, when it comes to resources to manage new (and sometimes exponential) growth, business owners fall into one of two camps: they either reactively throw more people at the problem (figuratively, of course) or they take on more and more of the workload themselves. Neither of these approaches is right and both effectively result in more work for the owner.

As difficult and time-consuming as it may be, this is when the owner needs to understand how things get done in the company and who is involved. This is achieved by The Gating Process™ from the previous section. It helps you map out what needs to be done, breaking these activities down into what is best done by the existing people in the team and what needs to be done by the owner of the business, and highlighting other activities that need to be done (but not by the current team or owner) that represent a gap in resources. Once this process is done effectively, then resources can be added exactly where they are needed and costs of increased headcount can be planned for.

Bridging The Capability Gap™ between the business owner and the next level in the company needs a fresh perspective as to what the company *could* look like from a resource and structure perspective if more experienced people are placed where they could add the most value. That kind of structure would add considerable value to the owner and make a positive difference to how the business is able to expand in a manageable way.

Employing a general manager to save the day

General managers (GMs) are very experienced and busy people. They have profit-and-loss accountability, they manage across multiple functions in the business, and they are more than capable of running a business day-to-day and putting structure and the right people in place.

However, make sure you don't delegate all responsibility to them. It is still your business and you still need to be across what is happening. You are still the leader.

Having said that, I know there are business owners who employ a general manager with a huge sense of relief and excitement. They think that, by putting that person in place, everything will take care of itself. That's not always how it works. In fact, you may *not* need a GM but, instead, one or two different people on your team who are capable of contributing far more.

Refer back to The Gating Process™ and ahead to the resource-mapping exercises later in this section before deciding that one person will change everything and be the right choice for now. Just remember not to expect everything from one person as the company expands.

Delegating because people are 'there'

Ineffective delegation is another mistake that can be made as a business grows. This is also not the right decision for the resourcing and structure of your business and will not enable the business to grow.

Sometimes the people you have trusted are not capable of dealing with what you've delegated. They may not say anything for fear of letting you down, or simply because they don't know how to say, 'No, I can't do that'.

I once had a client who ran one of their several businesses on a system that required very detailed data to be entered about client projects. The CEO had delegated this task to one of his only three employees in that business at the time. The problem was that this person was no more able to do this work than the CEO was – they didn't have the right experience or skill set. By the time I started helping them, this business was a mess. I discovered in a session with the teary employee that he had been struggling so much and knew he'd messed up but was afraid to speak up and tell the CEO.

I was able to help them address this problem. We brought in a tech expert from the system supplier to sort out what had been entered and clean it up, we documented how to use the system and we handed it over to one of the other team members, who was quite happy and able to do this role. Then, we reconfigured jobs and responsibilities to enable these changes to work effectively.

Business owners continuing to delegate more and more to long-standing employees – often their first employees who have been there since the beginning – is fraught with danger. Just because someone is in your business doesn't mean you can delegate anything and everything to them. There are levels of experience and capability that need to be assessed, just like you would a potential new employee. Don't delegate the wrong things to your existing people just because they're there.

Resource mapping

As a business grows into a better-structured entity, it is important to not only map out the resources you need, both now and further down the track, but do that in line with your own role as leader. If your plan is to grow turnover beyond low seven figures, you will need to relinquish control of some of the roles and activities you are currently holding onto to make way for responsibilities that are more in alignment with your role as CEO.

The goal is not to fall into the trap of The Capability Gap™ and to recruit the best and most capable people you can.

The best part of working through the exercise in table 6.6 is that it makes visible just how much (or how little) is being done by the people in your team.

The specific activities and responsibilities listed can be easily customised to the functions in your own business. The functions listed here are examples only to help you get started – you will need to adapt them for your own business.

Include whatever is relevant and delete what doesn't apply. You may prefer to use a mind map instead, which is an excellent tool to map out the key functional areas and associated responsibilities, but you will still need to answer questions in columns B through to I.

When I was helping a client plan for new resources and the roles that would be allocated to them, I had them do this exercise. I already knew what the outcome would be, but the visual impact of seeing the CEO's name in column B in just about every area of the company was the catalyst for the client to start mapping out new resources and a new team. The only things that my client *wasn't* doing were all the activities listed under the CEO role.

If you're finding it difficult to map out where you need support from new resources, start with this exercise.

Table 6.6: Identifying core functions and roles

A	B	C	D	E	F	G	H	I
Business function	**Who currently has responsibility for this within the company?**	**Does the CEO have to get involved here to get it done?**	**Is the current person responsible the best person to do it?**	**Could you move this activity to sit under another function?**	**Right now, could this be delegated to someone else or outsourced?**	**If you answered 'no' in column F, is there currently a resource gap here?**	**Do you need to recruit for a resource to do this?**	**Priority (High, Medium, Low)**
FINANCE & ADMIN (Overall)								
Budgeting & forecasts								
Cashflow management								
Managing external resources (accountants, auditors, etc.)								
Purchasing								
Accounts payable								
Accounts receivable / Invoicing								
Compliance (BAS, super, etc.)								
Managing third-party agreements: phones, insurances, internet, lease, etc.								
Management reporting								
Office admin: banking, mail, ordering, etc.								
Managing finance & admin team								
Day-to-day problem-solving								
Etc. – please add relevant functions for your business								

A	B	C	D	E	F	G	H	I
Business function	Who currently has responsibility for this within the company?	Does the CEO have to get involved here to get it done?	Is the current person responsible the best person to do it?	Could you move this activity to sit under another function?	Right now, could this be delegated to someone else or outsourced?	If you answered 'no' in column F, is there currently a resource gap here?	Do you need to recruit for a resource to do this?	Priority (High, Medium, Low)
SALES & MARKETING (Overall)								
Setting sales budgets								
Managing sales team/channels								
Running & interpreting sales reports								
Setting sales incentives & commissions								
Developing sales plan								
Developing marketing strategy								
Creating social media content								
Posting social media content								
Brand management								
Product development								
New business development								
Account management & service								
Website design & updates								
Day-to-day problem-solving								
Etc. – please add relevant functions for your business								

A	B	C	D	E	F	G	H	I
Business function	Who currently has responsibility for this within the company?	Does the CEO have to get involved here to get it done?	Is the current person responsible the best person to do it?	Could you move this activity to sit under another function?	Right now, could this be delegated to someone else or outsourced?	If you answered 'no' in column F, is there currently a resource gap here?	Do you need to recruit for a resource to do this?	Priority (High, Medium, Low)
OPERATIONS (Overall)								
Production								
Warehouse & Stock Management: raw materials, components, finished goods, etc.								
Planning & scheduling								
Technical support								
Installation / Service delivery								
Managing operations team								
Reporting and KPI management across operations								
Day-to-day problem-solving								
Etc. – please add relevant functions for your business								
SERVICE DELIVERY								
Taking client briefs								
Developing approaches and client proposals								
Drafting initial designs								
Delivering consultations								
Creating internal briefs for team								
Etc. – please add relevant functions for your business								

A	B	C	D	E	F	G	H	I
Business function	Who currently has responsibility for this within the company?	Does the CEO have to get involved here to get it done?	Is the current person responsible the best person to do it?	Could you move this activity to sit under another function?	Right now, could this be delegated to someone else or outsourced?	If you answered 'no' in column F, is there currently a resource gap here?	Do you need to recruit for a resource to do this?	Priority (High, Medium, Low)
CEO ROLE								
Strategy development & goal setting								
Strategy execution – high-level								
Managing direct reports – one-on-one meetings								
Risk management								
Reviewing and drilling down into management reports and dashboards								
Setting KPIs for direct reports								
Board reporting and attendance								
High-level client presentations/ meetings								
Strategic business development								
Developing & maintaining industry relationships								
Etc. – please add relevant functions for your business								
IT SUPPORT								
QUALITY ASSURANCE								
HUMAN RESOURCES								
CUSTOMER SERVICE								

Dashboards

Put all the useful indicators of performance into a report or dashboard – manual or automated, depending on the software used in your business – and use it to give you control of what is going on and highlight immediately anything that needs addressing.

Your dashboard could be created on a spreadsheet with charts and numbers that you review on a regular basis. It could also be a large one-pager with a series of infographics. You could have several dashboards.

As an example, a high-level dashboard would have financial data – sales, margin, profit and comparison to budget for the month and year to date. It could include key dates for important payments, such as tax, superannuation and payment plans. It could include the dates for completion of price reviews or major contract renewals. It could also include the company's cash position and variance from the preceding month. When you know what is important to your business, it can go onto the dashboard as a reminder.

Decide what is most important in making your business run more efficiently and profitably, and track it. For example, your margins may have been falling. You respond with several initiatives, including price increases where applicable, a focus on selling more profitable products and services and a reduction in direct expenses. This would be something you would need to track to measure how those initiatives impact margin (see table 6.7 overleaf).

This dashboard shows the margin breakdown for the company's three product lines.

Product 1 had a low margin of 20% in the previous year, with a budget to reach 35% in the current year. It is tracking well, sitting at 30% year to date. Products 2 and 3 have much higher margins, and are above last year's levels and close to or above the budget margin figures for the current year.

The total margin being closer to Product 1's margins indicates a higher volume of sales from Product 1, which keeps the total margin lower than the margins for the other two products.

Table 6.7: Product profit margin dashboard example

YEAR TO DATE (CURRENT MONTH)			
Product	**Last year**	**Budget**	**Current**
Product 1	20%	35%	**30%**
Product 2	58%	60%	**61%**
Product 3	57%	60%	**58%**
TOTAL MARGIN	**31%**	**40%**	**34%**

The margin tracking summary can be part of the main dashboard. A customer relationship management (CRM) system will produce data in a more visual format than this but, even if you need to enter the data manually to start with, it will provide important information you will need on a regular basis.

Lead generation, conversions and resulting sales figures are all critical numbers to track in a sales and marketing dashboard (see table 6.8). These are only examples to start you thinking about what you may track and measure in your business.

Table 6.8: Lead generation, conversions and total sales dashboard example

	Target	**Actual**
Leads via website	50	61
Leads followed up	61	58
Conversions	40%	50%
TOTAL SALES	**$200,000**	**$230,000**

All of this data can be drilled down into in other reports to show more detail. However, initially, it's the high-level data you need as this will identify exceptions and variances that you need to know about and address. You can drill down from there as required.

When you have a leadership team in place, they will generate dashboard reports for their respective areas of responsibility in the business, such as operations, marketing, sales and human resources. Dashboards are the tools for every key person on your A-Team to track and be accountable for their area of responsibility. They provide the most accurate need-to-know information. Think of the dashboard on your car providing all the vital information you need for each journey. If you run out of petrol, or a tyre is punctured, or the battery drains, or a fuse goes, these indicators alert you to the dangers so you can take immediate action.

Identify and track the corresponding vital indicators you need to know about in your business to keep everything functioning smoothly and performing well.

Case Study: The Attention Seeker

The Attention Seeker is a relatively new company specialising in personal branding and LinkedIn marketing and is the creation of Stanley Henry. The Attention Seeker serves B2B companies wanting to expand their client base through scaling their reputation and personal brand on LinkedIn and, more recently, TikTok.

Stanley and I hadn't met prior to our interview but LinkedIn posts are a good way to get to know a person and their business, and that is what Stanley's business is all about. He is a passionate and intentional attention seeker whose business has scaled rapidly in its first few years, directly off the back of his own personal branding on LinkedIn.

The company has a most interesting backstory. All the textbooks will advise that creating a business around an identified need in the market is the best strategy before deciding to actually start a business. In my experience, most people don't do that. However, that is exactly how The Attention Seeker started.

Prior to starting his business, Stanley held a senior operations role in a hotel, so he was familiar with customer service, recruiting, training and managing a team, tracking and reporting on key performance indicators for the hotel, and optimising sales and occupancy rates. He decided it was time for something new, so he and his partner left Melbourne and moved back to Auckland. Not knowing what the 'something new' was, Stanley went on a networking spree every day for six months to talk to businesspeople and determine what the market needed and what value he could add.

Hit the ground running

As he explains it, the people he spoke to were good at what they did but not necessarily at business development. At the time, apparently there were few people in New Zealand who really knew how to use LinkedIn for business. Since most of Stanley's new 'coffee contacts' originated from LinkedIn, after six months of networking that became his new business and many of them his new clients.

The Attention Seeker grew extremely quickly in the first two years. Fueling growth was possibly the need for his clients to focus more on digital business development due to the pandemic and long periods of lockdown in many countries. That and Stanley's preparation work prior to establishing the business helped drive rapid growth. Within little more than two years, the team numbered 11 in Auckland and 9 in the Philippines, with plans for more additions to come.

The Attention Seeker is a classic example of being its own best case study as it clearly has first-rate expertise in building business opportunities via LinkedIn.

Processes and culture

As the business is growing, there is a strong focus on processes and culture, starting with the recruitment process. As Stanley says, in the hospitality industry, hotel kitchens run with military precision. You have to onboard an employee in an afternoon. The Attention Seeker has processes for client onboarding, service delivery and individual employee job processes, which Stanley had each member of his team design.

Recruitment starts with a tongue-in-cheek video that reflects their irreverent culture. Then, a three-stage process begins with a group interview designed to identify how individuals interact with each other. The next stage is to be interviewed by two members of the team, with the final interview being conducted by Stanley.

Once a candidate has passed through this screening process, it's onto onboarding, which is an interesting process. During the first month, they are encouraged to 'find their place' in the team, the process of which could be described as 'listen, learn, assimilate'. During the second month, they need to focus on becoming familiar with their role and how to do it, and document the processes related to executing their role. During the third month, they have to 'find one thing' they are responsible for and become the go-to person for that thing. After that, they are expected to perform and contribute.

Interestingly, one aspect of the business that was slower to convert to a process was the creation of strategy. Stanley still has strategic vision and plans tucked away in his head, but this is not surprising given that the team doubled in its third year. A focus on structure was essential to make sure the team was functional, effective and on-brand with The Attention Seeker culture.

Stanley's challenge now is to implement a process for how he engages the team in developing the company's strategy, executes it and is accountable for it. The way he sees it, how he handles this next step 'has to get him where he wants to go long-term'.

The CEO as sales manager

As Stanley tells the story of the company's early days, it is surprising to learn that business development didn't come naturally to him. A self-confessed introvert, he has learned to love relationship-building and developing new opportunities. That has been a major shift for him and he now loves the role.

As such, he refers to his position as 'just the sales manager' and the visionary for the company, as well as the coach and mentor. There are now other people in the business who look after day-to-day people management and operations, as well as clients, and even the accounts function is outsourced. Stanley loves the problem-solving aspect of client projects, while his team does the execution.

Cash in, cash out

Another typical challenge that comes with rapid growth and which needs to be managed extremely closely is cashflow. Stanley runs his own spreadsheet for cashflow and updates revenue and expense forecasts on a daily basis. With the addition of more senior roles in the business, he equates the cost of those roles with the number of new clients required to cover the additional expense – a good practice to ensure margins don't reduce and profitability doesn't fall.

Stanley's focus on business development and meeting with new contacts on a daily basis – still –gives him the confidence to forecast likely conversions from connections and new sales revenue.

He believes that, with better processes, The Attention Seeker could double its client work with the same number of people on the team. Efficiencies with processes are critical to any business and, with applied focus, can result in more cost-effective supply chain management, better margins and doing more without adding more people to the business. This deserves attention as a business goes through each new stage of growth.

Stanley's team is doing for The Attention Seeker what the company does for its clients. As I said earlier, The Attention Seeker is its own best example of how it delivers value to its clients.

Business lessons

- It's all about the people. The right people aligned around your company's culture, with the right attitude, will make the company successful.
- Make it predictable. Forecasting, forecasting, forecasting. Don't just focus on expenses but work toward making your sales and new business conversions more predictable.
- Build relationships. People do business with people. Enough said.

theattentionseeker.com

Case Study: Erase Aesthetic Services Group

This is the story of a service business expanding beyond local customers to national customers through the addition of a product-based company. Vivien Gardiner is Managing Director of Erase Aesthetic Services Group, which comprises a skincare clinic offering cosmetic medical, laser and skin rejuvenation services and a professional, medical-grade skincare product distribution business.

I first met Vivien when we both attended and graduated from the Australian Institute of Company Directors course. Vivien has extensive experience as an executive and a company director, but 25 years ago she was a theatre nurse and her husband a plastic and reconstructive surgeon. Their current business structure started with a clinic providing laser services. Laser was new technology at the time and Vivien's husband had the foresight to realise it would become a growth area in skincare.

They also had the foresight to find superior products that were not available outside the US at the time and become the master distributor to the Australian market. They have partnered with Jan Marini Skin Research (JMSR) since 2001.

Vivien explained that their business, incorporating the clinic as well as their product-based business, has evolved organically. In the early days, they learned as they went, spent money on the wrong things some of the time, and they needed consultants and advisors to help them.

In recent years, there have been huge advances in technology for lasers, injectables and deliverables of skincare options, with social media increasing the reach of these advances globally. The plethora of choices for consumers, alongside massive growth in skincare practitioners (both qualified and unqualified), has given rise to the need for education around products, services and practices. Erase only has specialist surgeons deliver injectables.

Time for a strategy reset

After having to close the clinic for two years as a result of COVID-19, Erase Aesthetic Services did a business reset. As Vivien explained, it was a time to pause and think strategically. Although their clinic was constrained by a geographic footprint, the response to their national distribution business during this time influenced their strategic direction.

The strategy reset became all about education: educating consumers about best practices, educating their clients in how to look after their skin, and educating their team. They also focused heavily on educating the skincare clinics and spas they supplied product to and ensured that, as these clinics and spas expanded, Erase would remain a key supplier and source of quality education and training to its teams.

As a result of the strategy reset, their team has grown, their business premises have expanded and they're building a bigger platform for future opportunities. Vivien says it's important to be ready when a market slump bounces back, as it always does.

Erase has been fortunate with its people strategy, unlike some other companies in different industries. The 'great resignation' since COVID-19 has seen people wanting lifestyle changes and a shift from corporate to small business for a big culture change. This shift has created opportunities for those who have expertise in this field, and it has enabled the business to reimagine and rebuild its team. The key, says Vivien, is to be patient. They are now recruiting on culture rather than salaries, and their team all know each other and work together rather than in silos.

She said one of their greatest achievements has been holding it all together over the years – to have continued to nurture the business and their team, and to have kept the business rather than sold it (and there have been approaches), in which case Vivien said their team would have been slaves to a listed entity and accountable to shareholders. They have 28 staff; some have been there since the company started.

They have a profit-share arrangement to reward their team when the business does well.

Technology is a vital enabler

Apart from people capability, technology and digital capability are critical to success in reaching and educating their clients for both the clinic and the product business.

In terms of managing growth, they regularly report on key metrics from within their management system: weekly sales reports, year-on-year comparisons, costs and the impact of foreign exchange fluctuations and logistics variations, and cashflow. Forecasting and account plans drive inventory stability and service capacity, and regular staff training to stay up to date with product and industry developments is important for service differentiation and client retention.

From here, Erase and JMSR are likely to see a shift in how people purchase products and services to become more budget-conscious. Through their focus on education and digital technology, Vivien expects to be able to capitalise on that for their next stage of growth.

Business lessons

- Be as proactive as possible with annual and six-monthly planning to map out expected growth and the associated people and technology resources required.
- Think about the back end of the business and plan the infrastructure you are going to need as you grow.
- Digitisation is key. As they have grown, there has been more focus on technology as an enabler for growth, and that is an ongoing process. To that end, Vivien says digital capability is an essential resource to have in your business.
- As a leader, humility is key as it helps you manage people better: a willingness to listen and respond accordingly is important.

- Since COVID-19 and the social and work changes it has brought, there are now so many things affecting businesses: supply chain shortages, logistics expenses and delays. We have to learn that 'it is what it is' and be less reactive to these challenges.
- Also important to the growth of their companies has been a more strategic and less ad hoc approach. The core strategic focus is simple: look after customers, look after the team and manage cashflow tightly.

erase.com.au
janmariniaustralia.com.au

Chapter 7

Develop and Lead

Developing capabilities and accountability in your A-Team – and, correspondingly, shifting your role from business owner to CEO – is critical for growth.

At this stage, you really need to have a team that is capable of running the business day-to-day, and taking ownership of their roles and all the responsibilities that go with them. It is about having the right people in the right roles, building depth and strength into the company culture and being able to step up as the CEO who trusts, supports, relies on and rewards the capable people on the A-Team (see figure 7.1 overleaf). When you have such a team in place, they will challenge you to be better.

Upscaling is not just about the business. The leader needs to upscale too.

Developing people capabilities enables the business owner to step up as the leader. The better the owner becomes at leading, the more capability will be developed and nurtured in the team as a result.

I know from my own experience that this shift into the CEO role is almost impossible without the A-Team and, when you have a capable and reliable management team, you can achieve just about anything you set your mind to. Don't try and run a growing business with inexperienced people: they won't provide the shift that your business needs to expand further.

Figure 7.1: Develop and lead

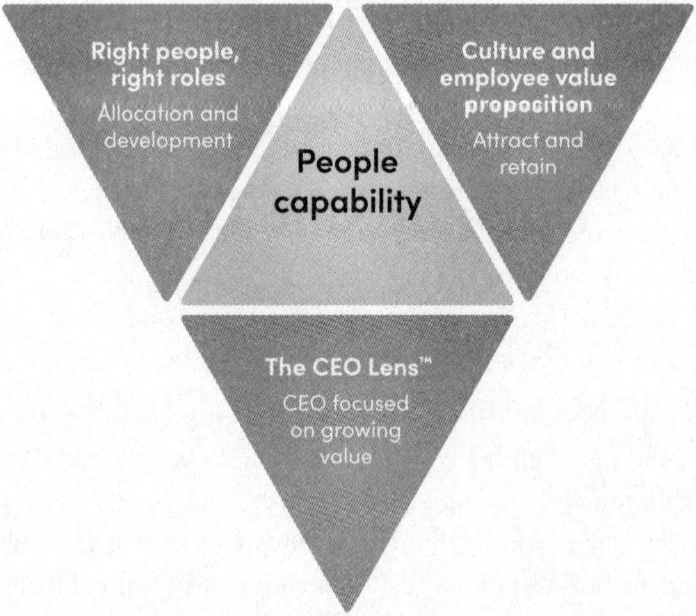

Your A-Team blueprint

The previous chapter looked at identifying resource gaps and filling them with capable people. This chapter is all about how to structure your team so you can step up as the CEO and lead them and the company. They are your A-Team and will enable you to fully step into a more strategic leadership role so, as a united team, you can drive the business forward.

Assemble

Someone once asked me: 'What makes someone part of your "A-Team"?' Without missing a beat, I suddenly (and unexpectedly) thought of King Arthur and the Knights of the Round Table. I replied that my 'A-Team' were like the Knights: unified, effective, loyal.

They ride alongside you; they follow your leadership; they protect you when necessary. They are 100% your best team.

In the 21st century, knights are all ages and sexes. It's not the gender of the knight that is important: it's the heart and soul.

If only more CEOs had a loyal, capable and reliable team to fully support them as they lead their companies. Finding and successfully managing this team has to be one of the greatest challenges of a CEO.

Too often, I see roadblocks that inhibit CEOs from finding and retaining their A-Team. Failure to overcome these blocks means you will fail to grow your business and your own role as CEO will never fully develop and grow.

If your direct reports are the right people – capable, loyal, committed to results, unified – you can achieve great things in your business. When you face a challenge or a crisis, these key people will be right there with you, helping to solve it. You won't be able to make it all the way on your own.

Remember, King Arthur didn't just let any old soldier in a metal skirt and a breastplate into his inner sanctum! *They* had to earn the privilege, but *he* had to see the potential.

How you assemble your team is important. Who and what will each person be responsible for?

When looking at the *role*, the best question to ask is, *Would the role be changed or reworked in any way if the current person in that role were removed?* If the answer is affirmative, then perhaps it is no longer the 'right' role and needs changing or removing.

When looking at the *person*, always ask, *If we didn't have a specific role for this person, would we still want them in the business somewhere?*

Categorise people and roles according to the matrix in figure 7.2 (overleaf).

Sometimes, when someone has been in the same role 'forever', we can be inclined to believe that the role is essential to the day-to-day functioning of the business when it isn't. If this situation exists in your company, it is time to reassess.

Figure 7.2: Right person, right role matrix

Right person, wrong role People in these roles have potential but may have been recruited for the wrong role. Rework resource-mapping exercise to identify if they can be redeployed.	**Right person, right role** The ideal situation: productivity is optimised and there is a cultural fit with the business.
Wrong person, wrong role Often a legacy issue. Both person and role need to be removed.	**Wrong person, right role** Remove and replace the person. The role is required but they aren't the right fit.

Often, we tell ourselves that chaos would ensue if certain people were to leave the company! It won't. Roles can be reconfigured, automated, completely changed or removed. People can be removed or reassigned and new roles can be created for people who could potentially add a lot of value to a business.

Specifically, when assessing if someone is the right person, I look at four key criteria (see table 7.1):

1. **Experience:** whether they have the skills and expertise to perform the role
2. **Attitude:** whether they will perform the role to the standard required
3. **Culture:** whether they even want to perform the role within the business
4. **Leadership:** whether they will help others to perform their own roles.

Each of these criteria is important and will help you define whether you have the right person.

When assessing whether a role is still right for the company, you need to ask four key questions (see table 7.1):

1. Does the company still need the role, or has it been changed or reconfigured or melded into other roles so that it may no longer exist?
2. Is there a purpose for having that role in the business and has it been clearly defined in scope?
3. Can the responsibilities of the role be quantified and, therefore, measured?
4. Can the responsibilities of the role be aligned to less tangible but equally as important qualifiable measures?

Table 7.1: Right people, right roles

Right people		Right roles	
✓	**Experience:** *can* they do it?	✓	Does the company need the role?
✓	**Attitude:** *will* they do it?	✓	Clear scope of purpose and responsibilities for role?
✓	**Culture:** do they *want* to do it with us?	✓	Clear accountabilities – quantifiable?
✓	**Leadership:** will they *help others* do it?	✓	Clear accountabilities – qualifiable?

Use the resource map (table 6.6, chapter 6) to group responsibilities together, and remove those activities from your own role that you should no longer be doing, to identify who and what key people in your team will be responsible for.

Once you have assembled your team to take on all of the activities of the company outside of the CEO role, you have the foundations of your A-Team.

Your direct reports should manage all aspects of the company between them. You ideally don't want any more than five. If your business is still relatively small, and depending on the business model, you could have as few as two.

At one point in my career, I had *18* direct reports. It was completely untenable. With too many direct reports, you aren't assembling your team in an efficient way. You become so busy managing these people that you have little time for anything else. Fewer direct reports means more time to attend to what you need to do in your own role.

Once your A-Team is in place, it's time to look to the future. You may have a consulting firm with $2.1M in turnover, and a budget of $2.8M for the next year and $4M the year after. What is your strategy for getting there? Will you be forming new alliances or targeting large new prospective clients, or are you focused on developing an app that will provide a major competitive edge and help bring on many more new clients? Who do you need in your team to help the business achieve those targets? Even if some of your resources are outsourced, you still need someone on your team to manage them.

If there are currently some key people who are your direct reports but you know they won't make it to the level of a knight, make sure you don't elevate their title above the role they are doing today. Say you have three direct reports today – it is more than likely they will all report into a more senior person in two years' time; at that point, that senior person becomes your direct report.

You obviously don't need to do anything more than think about how your resource needs may evolve as you grow, which impacts how you assemble the team around you today.

Assimilate

Building your culture and assimilating your team into it is a major element of your A-Team blueprint. A healthy and positive culture will enable your team to flourish, and will attract and retain new talent as the business expands. It is more critical now than ever before to be mindful of health and safety, mental health, employee happiness and satisfaction, and employees seeking options to find better workplaces.

There are companies in which culture is of no interest to the business owner. These companies are usually out of control, with an out-of-control owner, and employee churn is a big problem. No sooner are people onboarded into the company, they are running out the door and away from a toxic culture.

Companies who invest in culture are so refreshing. They work hard at it, they focus on it and they really value it, and they have productive and effective teams as a result. Employee attrition is low.

Two of the greatest challenges for all businesses are people retention – and at costs the business can afford – and being able to attract new people. It's important to do an 'employee reality check' (see figure 7.3) so you have the insights to be able to attract, engage and retain your key people. If a refresh of any part of your team is required, you need to be across this as well.

Figure 7.3: Employee reality check

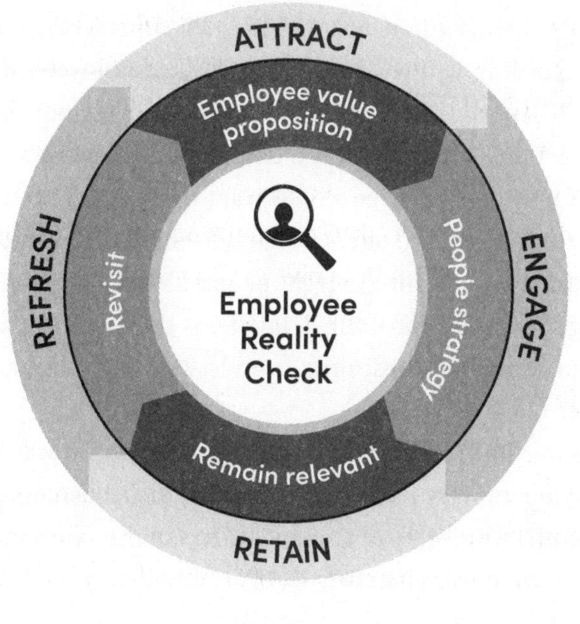

At the heart of this model is the employee value proposition (EVP). The purpose of using this tool is to help drive a positive culture, attract the right people and ensure that what you are providing stays relevant to your team.

The EVP is created from the feedback that is provided by your team in a structured way. With this feedback, you will have the insights you need to develop a 'people strategy'. This basically outlines your company's recruitment guidelines, the onboarding process, tangible rewards and intangible benefits for your team, and retention and career development strategies. It's all about attracting, retaining and developing your people within a positive cultural framework.

This exercise can be conducted annually if the size and growth of your team warrants it. It is an ideal tool if you sense there may be problems with your people and culture. It is also valuable for large teams to enable the leader to get closer to what everyone is really thinking and feeling. It is best done face-to-face in order to extract more detailed and valuable feedback. It can also be done with certain apps – although the level of feedback is generally not as deep, this method is more efficient for large teams.

An EVP is the new non-negotiable when considering your people strategy. According to PwC research of 1800 employees, a company 'that doesn't have an employee value proposition is not going to be able to attract and retain critical talent'. An EVP answers the simple question of why an employee would want to work for your company over other alternatives and offers. What is the EVP your company offers that will attract and retain the right people? While the PwC research targets larger organisations, the principle is definitely applicable and beneficial to companies upscaling from low seven figures and toward eight figures.

In the same PwC study, perhaps not surprisingly, it was found that 38% of employees were planning on leaving their business within the next 12 months while 48% of C-suite leaders in the same business had no plans to adjust or revisit their EVP.

There can clearly be a big disconnect between what people want from their company and how well they think it is being delivered, and what the leadership team thinks they want. That disconnect needs to be addressed if companies are to retain their existing talent and be competitive enough to attract new people to the business. Contractors and outsourced resources are also part of this mix, so EVP has a wide reach.

So, what do companies need to consider when assessing their EVP? What are some of the factors that their people value? How highly do employees value these factors?

Business owners and leaders need to be mindful – particularly in smaller businesses that don't have endless funds to lure new talent and retain existing talent – that understanding the motivations and fundamental needs of employees is essential. The best way to do that is to approach the team in a very objective and structured way to uncover what they value most in an employer and what would make them stay or leave, and ask them to score the business on a number of values applicable to today's working environment.

In many cases, people leave because they can't see future development or career paths. However, when an employee can't see the next position for them in the company (or the next spot in the organisation chart), what they are missing is that growth and development doesn't need to be up a vertical hierarchy. This is particularly true in small companies. Extended roles, greater responsibility, increased remuneration and bigger titles worthy of the work they are doing all constitute career progression, even if the employee can't 'see' this ongoing opportunity at the time. If your team understood the real potential for progression and development in your business, they would no doubt stay in your business for longer. Just because a role doesn't seem to exist today doesn't mean they couldn't be owning it in the future.

People are also attracted to – or leave – companies because of the culture. Culture, of course, incorporates a wide array of factors such as purpose, values, leadership, respect, communication and behaviour.

Today, we also need to factor in flexibility. How important are all these factors to your people, and why?

According to Gartner research of 5000 employees conducted in 2021, the traditional approach to EVP focuses too much on what the company *gives* the employee rather than *why*. The research concludes that value comes from feelings, not features. I think this point is critical. How does working for your company make your people *feel*?

In a 2019 article on builtin.com (and updated in 2022), Kate Heinz found that 46% of job seekers cite company culture as 'very important' when choosing to apply to a company. Likewise, 47% of active job seekers cite company culture as the primary reason they are looking for work elsewhere.

When you dig deeper, you get the gold that will really help improve your company's EVP. In my experience, when given the opportunity, people will share honestly and in detail what they love about a company and what they feel could be improved. There are two levels of feedback: the emotional level and the more objective level. Some feedback is relatively easy to address; other adjustments will require a bigger shift in the company and how it is run. Culture is the big overarching challenge for business owners and leaders, and how it makes people feel seems to be the most important factor to get right.

There are other important factors to consider in this EVP mix and only your team can articulate what they are.

If your company is going to manage people challenges, the development of an appropriate strategy to align your team's values with those of the business is essential.

It's all well and good to have independent, in-depth interviews with your team to uncover their perceptions, preferences and non-negotiables, but you need to decide as a business what *your* preferences and non-negotiables are, because there does need to be a balancing act. In summary, here is a quick overview of the steps to take to ensure your EVP works well for your people and your business, particularly if you need to make adjustments in your business:

1. Ideally, *have an independent person conduct your team interviews.* You will receive more in-depth and useful information because questions will be structured in a way that extracts more feedback, and your team will generally be more comfortable with someone who isn't a colleague.
2. By having a structured process, you will be able to *put measures around the most important factors* in your company's EVP. You must be able to measure what you are assessing to create a benchmark for future development. For example, your team wants 'better communication': what does that really mean and how can improvements be measured?
3. Decide whether you have any *non-negotiables* in your business – for example, the number of days working in the office, or annual leave accruals.
4. *Present your findings* to the team. You need to be transparent with this exercise and continue to engage them once they have taken the time to provide their feedback, insights and ideas.
5. You need to *tell your team what you are going to do* to enhance your company's EVP and their experience of being part of the company.
6. *Provide an implementation plan.* Engage key team members in this process as appropriate (discuss with them first) and get things in motion. As the leader, it is essential that you are the driver of this process.
7. *Be prepared to negotiate.* Go back to point 3 and know what your non-negotiables are. People need to be paid for their contribution and value and given recognition for good performance. On the flipside, remember that no-one is indispensable. If you can no longer meet remuneration demands, you will have to be prepared for people to leave. It is a cycle, after all.
8. Finally, *you must deliver*. All of this is pointless, and highly counterproductive, if you fail to follow through. Enough said.

Even in a tight market, there's always more than one plan you can follow, and attracting and retaining the right talent is a cycle. A strong EVP will help give you a competitive edge in the talent challenge.

Before wrapping up this section, I want to make special mention of building remote teams. When you have a business in a single location, it takes work to get in place the right team, culture, company processes, communication, workflow, exception reporting when things go pear-shaped, and structure. Add people in other states or countries into the mix, particularly when there is one physical office, and the dynamic changes. Recruitment criteria for those team members who are in a remote location and working from home, mentoring and development, remote implementation of the necessary IT and systems, clear processes and effective team communication become even more important and difficult to make effective for the remote employees.

Remote teams need a home

My personal belief from having run teams in 'remote' locations – most employes were in an office space but some worked from home – is that it is essential for the leader, at least, to go to these remote locations and visit the team (and the customers, if applicable). It is also beneficial – depending on the size of the remote team and if the business can afford it – to have a local country team leader as the first point of contact to give the team a stronger sense of belonging. They can then meet locally in person more easily and also get together as a group annually.

As a company grows, more focus on communication at all levels is essential to keep the team growing together. Being vigilant about new recruits will ensure maintenance of the quality of the A-Team – don't let anyone through the net if they don't fit with the culture, regardless of their role or location.

Align

Once you have your A-Team and positive culture in place, it's important to ensure that your people and your company goals are in alignment.

When I work with clients to help them upscale from seven to eight figures, they already have good businesses and some structure in place. But a sub-$2M company will have less complexity than a $10M company and, as the business grows, there are more measures that need to be tracked.

Apart from the overall business numbers in the P&L and balance sheet, there needs to be correlation and alignment between your business KPIs and those for functional areas and individuals. For example, if the business goal is to reach $8.5M in sales, then the targets for the sales team need to correlate directly with that number.

Here's how to determine KPIs for other areas of the business and the people working in those areas (production, operations or customer service for example):

1. Start by asking what the key outcomes are that you want to achieve for that area. For example, a strategic focus for a company may be retention of all major clients (perhaps because they have had some attrition). Account managers will be driven by KPIs for

customer retention, customer satisfaction and probably customer value. Operations could be measured against production and delivery of physical product and provision of support services. Customer service could focus on indicators such as customer resolution rates (for example, 100% of problems resolved on the first call), and it could report on green, orange and red categories of outstanding customer issues and apply a percentage to each.

2. Ask, *What is an acceptable number/rate/score if we are to achieve our overall targets?*
3. Align the KPIs of the people responsible for those metrics with the numbers themselves. For example, whoever is responsible for customer service is responsible for keeping customer service KPI numbers within acceptable levels.
4. Then, allocate individual KPIs to the people in your team responsible for each of the activities that drive the numbers. For example, a customer service team member may be responsible for providing first-level response to all customer calls within two hours.

If you start with your high-level company goals and targets and then break it down, you can have measures set up across the business, and you can know by looking at the dashboards how well you are tracking and what exceptions may need urgent attention.

The CEO Lens™

It isn't easy making the shift from business owner to CEO. This is the shift from being involved in running your business day-to-day to taking a step back and up, entrusting daily operational management to a capable team while you focus on the responsibilities of a CEO.

I use the term The CEO Lens™ to help business owners understand what is involved in making this shift. I think it's more powerful and inspirational than a position description.

First, I want to provide some context by exploring what I see as the four key roles of a CEO. These concepts may be familiar or new to you depending on how far you have gone in making this shift in your own business.

All CEOs have a first time in the role. In most seven-figure companies where the founder runs the business, they have never been a CEO before, and many of them haven't had executive roles working in other companies. As such, they don't have reference points as they navigate from low seven figures and toward eight figures. Very few people understand what a CEO does, even those who need to step into the role in their own company.

They are used to being involved in everything and often trying to control everything. As the business grows, this approach is untenable. I heard a title for how business owners operate at this stage that I think is very apt: 'Chief Everything Officer'.

One of the main components of the Shift Business Growth Framework™ for upscaling growth is the Develop and Lead component, so understanding what the CEO role entails is important. It isn't easy to make the shift but it is essential if you want to grow your company beyond $2M and toward eight figures.

1. Create the vision

What drives you forward? What is the picture you can see for your business?

A vision unfolds in the owner's head. When you first start out, unless you're Richard Branson or Elon Musk, you probably have goals rather than a vision. There might be a hazy picture of where you want to take the business but, in the beginning, the focus has to be on take-off.

Once the business is viable and has a team, the CEO must make the vision clear for everyone. That means they need to get it out of their head and communicate it clearly to the team.

The vision provides strategic direction, from which come the priorities of the whole team. The vision makes it clear to your team, customers and partners what your business is about, what is stands for, who it serves and the value it delivers.

Here are a few examples from businesses that once were small (taken directly from their websites):

- Carman's. Our vision is to be the most loved Australian gourmet food brand, enjoyed every day, around the world. Everything we do flows from that.
- Apple: To make the best products on earth and to leave the world better than we found it.
- Disney: To be one of the world's leading producers and providers of entertainment and information.
- Amazon: Our vision is to be Earth's most customer-centric company, where customers can find and discover anything they might want to buy online, and endeavours to offer its customers the lowest possible prices.

These are big vision statements from organisations operating (to different degrees) on a global basis. Clearly, considerable thinking has gone into the specific words used to craft such specific visions. If the vision has been well-crafted then, like Carman's vision statement says, 'everything we do flows from that'.

Driving and helping to craft the vision statement is a core component of The CEO Lens™.

2. Be the conductor

Think of the vision as the symphony. The strategy and action plan is the sheet music. Your team is the orchestra, with everyone focused on doing their bit for the whole. The CEO is the conductor bringing it all together.

The conductor doesn't play any instrument in the orchestra (although they may be able to, and to do it well!). The conductor can hear what is working and what needs tweaking. They know what to do to get the whole orchestra playing in harmony.

There can only be one conductor for the orchestra to follow. The conductor must keep everyone on track with the sheet music, on tempo and all working together to achieve the right balance.

The conductor doesn't rush in and grab an instrument from someone who isn't playing as well as they need to. No, they have their own job to do: to lead and get the best from their orchestra. If they are a good conductor, their people will follow.

That is the role of the CEO – to be the conductor and lead your team. In order to do that, you need to know your team and their capabilities, what makes them respond and lift their game, and what will demotivate them. You need to be able to allocate the right instruments to the right people and lead them in formation toward the company's vision.

They need to trust you. They need to trust your capabilities and your judgement, and that you have their back. These are the characteristics and capabilities that you need to embody as the conductor.

3. Steer the company

Strategic decisions that impact the progress of the company fall to the CEO. You need to know how to make these decisions. In the next chapter I refer to the 'strategic foundations' that underpin a company's growth. They also provide guidance, direction and criteria against which decisions can be made.

If you follow the principles in this book, you will have the best quantitative and qualitative information you need to steer your company, including data analysis, research and cultural parameters.

In the event of unchartered waters, such as a pandemic, you need to continue to be the conductor, hold onto the vision and lead through the challenge in the same way you would want to be led if you weren't the CEO. As long as you have the numbers and a dashboard, and the right people, you will be able to steer and course-correct from wherever you are. Don't ignore the dashboard, engage in regular two-way communication with your team, customers and key stakeholders, and try to stay calm and think. You can't steer if you remain too deeply in the day-to-day and never look up to see where the company is actually headed.

This is a major shift for many business owners and, if you want to make it into The 7% Club, it is essential to master.

4. Take full responsibility for decisions and results

This should go without saying but, unfortunately, there are still CEOs who operate with a focus on blame. It is unacceptable to blame anyone in your team for decisions or results that didn't go according to plan.

If I hear someone blaming their team for poor company performance, missed opportunities or mistakes that lost the company a client, all I hear is warning bells. This person has failed to see their business through The CEO Lens™. They are also creating a negative and possibly toxic culture through their behaviour.

Mistakes will always happen, and it is the CEO's role to first take responsibility for what has happened and deal with it, and then to try and ensure it doesn't happen again. Mistakes are *usually* the result of a process issue or a people issue.

Decisions that were wrong and results that aren't achieved may be due to several reasons, but the role of the CEO is to take full responsibility and deal with them. If you are a director of a company, you cannot claim ignorance as a defence. A director has responsibility to stay across the numbers, core activities and initiatives in a business, and ask questions to uncover more depth of information or to explore anomalies. As the CEO, the same applies.

*

Once your business structure and team are in place, it's time to focus on you and what you will be looking at through The CEO Lens™.

You need the qualities that will allow you to lead your people and build culture, and steer the company and make strategic decisions that progress you toward the company's vision. As you can see with the CEOs interviewed throughout this book, people and culture are a priority focus for all of them – good people will help grow the business the right way.

Here are the focus areas for you, as CEO, that can add the most value to your business while letting your team take care of the day-to-day:

- being the leader
- business strategy
- creation of value
- culture
- key relationships.

These factors speak for themselves, and I see them as the more visionary and expansive aspects of The CEO Lens™. Other people in the business may be involved in some or all of these activities, depending on their roles, but it is these activities that the CEO will focus on as the core part of their role.

The role of 'leader' will certainly evolve over time. What does **being the leader** mean?

Earlier in this chapter I talked about the four key roles of a CEO. Being the leader means that your team will follow you (and be your knights) if you *enable* them. You need to help them develop and grow so they can fully contribute to the development of the business and experience their own fulfilment in the process. You need to treat people with compassion and understanding. You need to respond to mess-ups with questions, not blame, to understand what happened and how so you can address it appropriately.

The CEO must understand their own core competencies and how they can *best add value* to the business, and then go and do that.

You need to lead by example and with integrity. You need to be *reasonable* and *approachable*, otherwise your team will try to deal with exceptional challenges (that should have been escalated to you) on their own. You need to set *standards* and *boundaries* so your team knows what is and isn't acceptable with their own behaviours and accountability.

You can only lead when others want to follow you. It provides an interesting perspective to question whether *you* would follow yourself as the leader.

Business strategy and the **creation of value** are discussed in detail in chapter 6. They encompass the identification of opportunities for expansion. Looking through The CEO Lens™, you will see opportunities in many places: new products and services, serving new niche markets, aligning with strategic partners to develop new business, dominating a niche through specialising in products or services for companies in that niche, implementing technology to gain a competitive advantage, identifying gaps and finding potential to remove competitors in your market. Innovation and technology are part of the company's strategy, as are all functional areas of the business that will be central to the implementation of strategy. While the team will be responsible for execution, it is the CEO's responsibility to drive this and always be looking through The CEO Lens™ in a strategic way to gain advantage for the business.

Culture needs to be driven and monitored by the CEO, who is the guardian of company culture. If there is a culture of the team feeling instant relief as soon as you leave the building and take the negative vibes with you, this is your problem. You cannot complain about your people if you do nothing to improve the situation.

When you look through the CEO Lens™, you will see not just individuals but the culture permeating through your organisation. This is important as it is the cohesion that binds them and your company together. Maintaining and nurturing that is your ultimate responsibility.

It is also important that the CEO role maintains a focus on **key relationships**. Staying close to customers and occupying a position as a valued partner not only provides potential opportunities for growth but protects one of your most important assets. Relationships with important suppliers will help protect the company's ongoing supply of services and/or raw materials in tight markets. Strong industry relationships are important for new business opportunities and to stay across trends as they are emerging, as are relationships with competitors (as appropriate) for potential future acquisition or collaboration. For the CEO, the focus of these relationships will always be to help deliver advantage in some way to the company, as well as to position the business as a preferred employer wherever possible.

These other items you will see through your lens are more about management and steering the company:

- monitoring and tracking company dashboards
- cashflow management and KPIs for the company and the people in it
- risk assessment and management
- commercial protection.

As you can see, this is a very different perspective than that of an operational business owner.

The CEO Lens™ is a tool to help you shift your focus from 'doing' activities to 'leading' activities as you grow your company. It requires a big shift to get to this point but, once there, you will never go back. You will have become the leader your team and your business needs.

One more thing about you as the leader: it helps to have the capability to empathise, listen, consider different perspectives, think before reacting, show maturity, be authentic, have fun and laugh while still leading, mentor and help develop your team, be humble and be kind. For some, this comes naturally; for others, less so. But, if you focus on this aspect of The CEO Lens™, you will get better at it. Your team will notice and respond positively.

When you learn to develop your team and step up as the leader, creating and implementing the strategies to upscale your business will be so much easier.

Case Study: Content 10x

Founded by Amy Woods, Content 10x is a specialist content creation agency based in the UK. I find Amy's story interesting as her sizeable and growing team all work from home in different parts of the UK and the Philippines, and her approach to growth is to make it manageable as the business continues to expand.

Talking with Amy was most engaging, not just because of the enthusiasm she has for her growing company but also because of her lilting Irish-British accent!

Unlike some other companies in The 7% Club profiled in this book, Amy's business has only been in operation a relatively short period of time (at the time of writing). In five years she took her startup agency from 0 to 12 employees. Her model of a virtual agency with team members working from anywhere in the world has had rapid growth, bringing both success and some interesting challenges.

Initially, Amy worked with freelancers to help deliver services, but when she secured her first retainer client she recruited her first employee after only a few months. The business took off from there. With content marketing being such a critical component of any marketing campaign, the demand for these services is climbing.

In terms of promoting her business and brand, Amy was and still is the front person. She is heavily involved in delivering talks and keynotes at industry events and, of course, given her company's expertise she has an active profile through their own content repurposing.

Addressing the challenges of going virtual

The growing team now numbers 14, scattered throughout the UK mostly, with the creative team based in the Philippines. Content 10x is now facing a different kind of challenge with people and culture. Pre-pandemic, they were a virtual agency, with employees able to work from anywhere. It was a different business model, and was embraced by their team and attractive to new recruits. Now, this virtual model is more familiar and no longer special and enticing. The challenge facing Amy in this post-pandemic market is that new team members want a hybrid arrangement – to be able to have an office to go to when they want or need to as well as having the flexibility to work from home. As Amy says, it is almost impossible to find a physical head office location that will suit all of the team given their dispersed geographic locations. Her plan is to continue with the remote business model.

It's a balancing act, trusting your team when they work remotely and have minimal in-person contact with you or the rest of their colleagues. Zoom calls, as common as they are, fail to enable us to pick up on nuances and cues that we would easily notice in person. Dissatisfaction, disengagement, disagreement – all of these are more difficult to monitor when the working relationship you have with your team is distant.

This is why culture is Amy's primary focus, as it is even more important to monitor and foster as geographic working distances increase.

Her approach to recruitment is aimed at addressing some of the challenges of a dispersed team. Amy now screens potential candidates against additional criteria. For team members to work from home happily and productively without relying on face-to-face interaction with other team members, two factors are vitally important. The first is that they need to genuinely love what they do – that may sound obvious, but when you think about what it's like being in your 'zone' when doing the work you really love and are good at, you can imagine that it's less important having people around you. The second factor Amy has discovered is that it is important for her team to have interests outside of work – personal interests and activities help to balance the lack of social interaction they get from their work environment.

Not attending a physical office on a regular basis is absolutely perfect for many people – with no commuting, no work wardrobes and no office politics, it can be a dream situation for some. However, it's also not for everyone, so finding those who are genuinely comfortable with it is key.

Checking in on the Content 10x team on a regular one-on-one basis is critical. Everyone has a one-on-one with their line manager at least once per week. Team meetings are held via Zoom daily and weekly, and there are some monthly meetings too, with a lot of emphasis placed on making every person feel part of the team.

Amy brings the UK team together a few times a year and is considering options to bring the entire team together. It's important for everyone to have the opportunity to build on existing relationships by meeting their virtual colleagues in person.

Until that time, another immediate challenge has been the growing complexity in the business and the make-or-break tipping point for continued growth.

Stepping up as CEO

A couple of years ago, Amy was fortunate to bring on board an executive assistant from a public relations agency who also had experience in finance and administration. She took over a raft of responsibilities from Amy across finance, HR, recruitment, sales admin, team wellbeing and implementing processes, which enabled Amy to step back and up into the CEO role. To quote Amy, she 'grew up' when she was able to let go of the day-to-day and focus on leading and building the company.

A core part of Amy's role is sales and new business development (because she has always done this) and it is clear that she now needs someone else to focus on this too. In her words, she still doesn't have enough time to focus on strategic priorities.

As we discussed this in more detail, it became obvious to me that the gap between Amy's role and skill set and the rest of the team was too big. She needed to address The Capability Gap™. Amy is aware of this and is focused on closing the gap, having the right people in the right roles and having someone else to focus on sales and business development to free her up further to work more on, rather than in the detail of, the business.

As the company has grown, Amy has been able to make the shift into the CEO role. She has recognised that essential changes needed to be made to the focus of her own role, the level of support she needed from the right team, and processes and performance measures, enabling her to focus on strategy rather than daily operations.

Business lessons

- The most difficult challenge, without doubt, is making sure the people you bring onto your team are the right people. They need to be developed and nurtured and buy into what you are doing, your values and your brand. The most important things for growing your business are the right people in the right roles, a team that cares and happy clients.
- Financial goals are important but you need to get there in the right way. Your business needs to be manageable as you grow.
- Having someone in the business who can manage the day-to-day is a game changer. Being able to delegate that and focus instead on what you are meant to be doing as the leader is the turning point for really being able to grow your business.
- Processes are critical for delivering a high value and high-quality service.

content10x.com

Case Study: Total Beauty Network

Tony Rechtman is the Founder and Managing Director of Total Beauty Network. TBN is an example of how it is not unusual for business growth to span decades as seven figures becomes eight and then compounds over time.

When I arrive for our interview, I'm greeted by one of the team, who then races back to a team meeting. I can see a room full of people all standing. Apparently, this is a TBN tactic for making meetings shorter and more efficient. I know about standing desks, but standing meetings is an interesting new twist!

TBN is an award-winning producer of colour cosmetic and skin-care brands based on certified organic, certified vegan and certified cruelty-free formulations. TBN's distribution channels focus on pharmacy, beauty spas and online, as well as selected retailers in Australia and 30 international markets. Its brands are INIKA Organic, Designer Brands (DB), Colour by TBN and Raww Cosmetics.

It took Tony about eight years to reach eight figures. Growth since then has occurred much more rapidly, with 8 million products being sold annually. Tony has ambitious growth goals to 2030, with a target of 30 million products sold annually and revenue that tips into nine figures. The company has an impressive track record to date, so the next few years will be an interesting time for TBN and its team.

Early days

Tony was the sole employee when he started his business back in 2004 with DB. The focus was always pharmacy and the initial battle was to compete for shelf space against known high-end brands. DB had a solid value proposition of quality product at an affordable price and early supporters helped set the foundations for growth.

Like most founders, Tony was heavily involved in operations from day one, doing sales, product development, order-processing and pick and pack. Fortunately, the brand took off in pharmacy and the company's team grew in the first few years to 18.

As Tony says, in those days he had many challenges around growth. He sacrificed his own salary for five years to employ more salespeople to grow the business. There were always challenges around when to employ more people, where to put them and whether they could do multiple jobs to minimise cost and maximise growth potential. Tony always preferred to add salespeople rather than non-revenue-generating support people. It was a case of all hands on deck, as it is with most startups and growing small businesses.

In these early days the business made the shift from MYOB to SAP. After spending $250,000 on this exercise, Tony pulled the pin just before it went live. He didn't have the confidence that it would help his business. He says he still doubts this decision, but he isn't convinced he made the wrong decision either. His learning from that was to put in an off-the-shelf system and not try to customise it from day one.

Business growth is all about these sorts of decisions, where the answer and the decision-making criteria can be grey. It may work, it may not, it may be alright sometimes – the point is to make a decision, act on it and move forward. If you need to regroup, do so, but don't agonise over decisions. Keep moving.

Growing and trusting people

As with most business founders, Tony had to make the big shift from being hands-on in the everyday business to being the leader.

TBN today has over 100 people in the team, mostly in Australia but some offshore. Tony is still involved in the interview process, making sure people are a good fit.

His team love working from home two days a week and three in the office. As with any business in the current market, as natural attrition occurs and people leave, it is becoming harder to attract and recruit replacements. In order to find the best, they need to pay top dollar.

I have had many discussions with CEOs about this issue in recent times. One of the problems with paying top dollar when it is not commensurate with the actual experience of the employee is that employers have greater expectations of that person *because* they are effectively paying the salary of a more experienced person. Eventually, the person may fly in the role, but they are more likely to fail and leave.

Other CEOs favour attracting people from corporate environments to their smaller companies by offering more flexibility and more customised packages. If a business cannot afford top dollar to attract new employees, a compelling employee value proposition is critical, offering benefits that appeal to candidates more than top-dollar remuneration. As Fillr co-founder Chad Stephens explains later in this book, the value proposition for their team is more engagement in the plans and progress of the company, the opportunity to work with big-name tech clients and an employee share option plan. Vivien Gardiner offers her Erase Aesthetic Services team a more enjoyable cultural shift from corporate to smaller business, which is a big bonus for many, and a profit-share arrangement as well.

Tony told me that the next two years (at the time of writing) will be hard when it comes to finding the right talent at affordable salaries. Like many CEOs, he says that people issues are his greatest challenge. It is a natural evolution of growth that, the bigger the company grows, the more your structure will need experienced and specialised people, adding to headcount and expenses.

Like most founders, Tony struggled to let go when he employed an Office Manager. He kept trying to do what he employed her to do. After her fourth remonstration telling him, 'You have to let go', she told him she was leaving. He let go. She stayed. Familiar story!

As Tony says, you have to trust people and give them training and guidance, and know that, if you have the right people and the right culture, your team will do their very best. That is a huge shift for a CEO.

Strategic expansion

TBN has pursued many opportunities presented over the last few years and, of course, some were more profitable than others. These days it has narrowed its focus to three priorities per quarter. That has forced it to assess different opportunities and focus on which will have the biggest impact.

The leadership team is involved in strategic planning. Growth has to be profitable and, as the owner of the company, Tony thinks about questions like *When is enough enough?*, *What are our next big goals?* and *Who do I want around me?*

TBN's brands are based on a philosophy of helping the planet and their customers, and it is important for TBN's team members to like and believe in what they are doing. As Tony says, when you are doing things for the right reasons, the financial impact will follow.

That sounds like a perfect 'why' to persevere in reaching eight figures and beyond!

Business lessons

- People won't pay you, people will leave, customers will go broke – don't take it personally.
- Back yourself.
- Trust your gut.
- Having the right people doing the right things at the right times is essential.
- Take advice from others but make your own decisions.
- Self-belief is essential.

tbn.com.au

Chapter 8

Strategise and Scale

Strategic planning at a corporate level is very different from the process set out here. For more nimble, privately held small businesses with a growing team, it's critical to have an overarching vision and purpose to help you stay on track and give everyone an understanding of what you are all working toward. Clear goals and an action plan to achieve them that keeps everyone accountable is essential. In order to get there, the process needs to be clear, adaptable and easy to follow.

Before you start, keep these considerations in mind:

- **Do not set yourself up to fail:** For example, if it has taken you ten years to reach $8M in turnover, don't set a goal to double sales in the next 12 months – not impossible but highly unlikely.
- **Engage your team in the process:** They will be accountable for helping to execute the strategy. As the CEO you may have the high-level vision for where you are taking the company but you still need to engage your key people and get their input.
- **Prepare:** Do your research. Know what assumptions you are making about the market, your clients and your business. It takes some time but it is worthwhile and the difference between a viable strategy and a hopeful one.

Having a strategy roadmap is critical if you want to upscale. You need to understand the landscape you're in and the opportunities and gaps.

I have discovered that a lot of business owners are unsure how to go about creating a strategy roadmap for their company. They aren't sure whether or not to include their team in the process and they don't know what the plan should contain. Many have not done the analysis of their business to really understand how well it is performing and what is happening beyond their business that represents growth opportunities. They tend to either ignore the significance of their competitors or obsess about them! Unfortunately, some fail to have deep and insightful conversations with their customers. Often, technology is not front and centre in the strategic mix in terms of enabling upscaling and efficiency. All of these elements are important for creating a strategy that will enable you to achieve your growth goals.

This chapter will set out the process as simply as possible, so getting started and creating that all-important strategy roadmap will be easy. If you follow this process, the end result will be a strategy roadmap to take your business into The 7% Club!

The process

There are basically five sections to creating your strategy roadmap:

1. **Strategic foundations:** these underpin your business
2. **Business situation, insights and opportunities:** explore the business and its environment
3. **Goals and strategic priorities:** these need to be aligned
4. **Focus areas:** these are the key actions to achieve goals in the next 12 months
5. **Actions and accountabilities:** these provide the detail of the action plan.

You can start this process at step 1 or 2 – both are part of the *preparation* required for The Strategy Roadmap™ (see figure 8.1).

Figure 8.1: Process to develop The Strategy Roadmap™

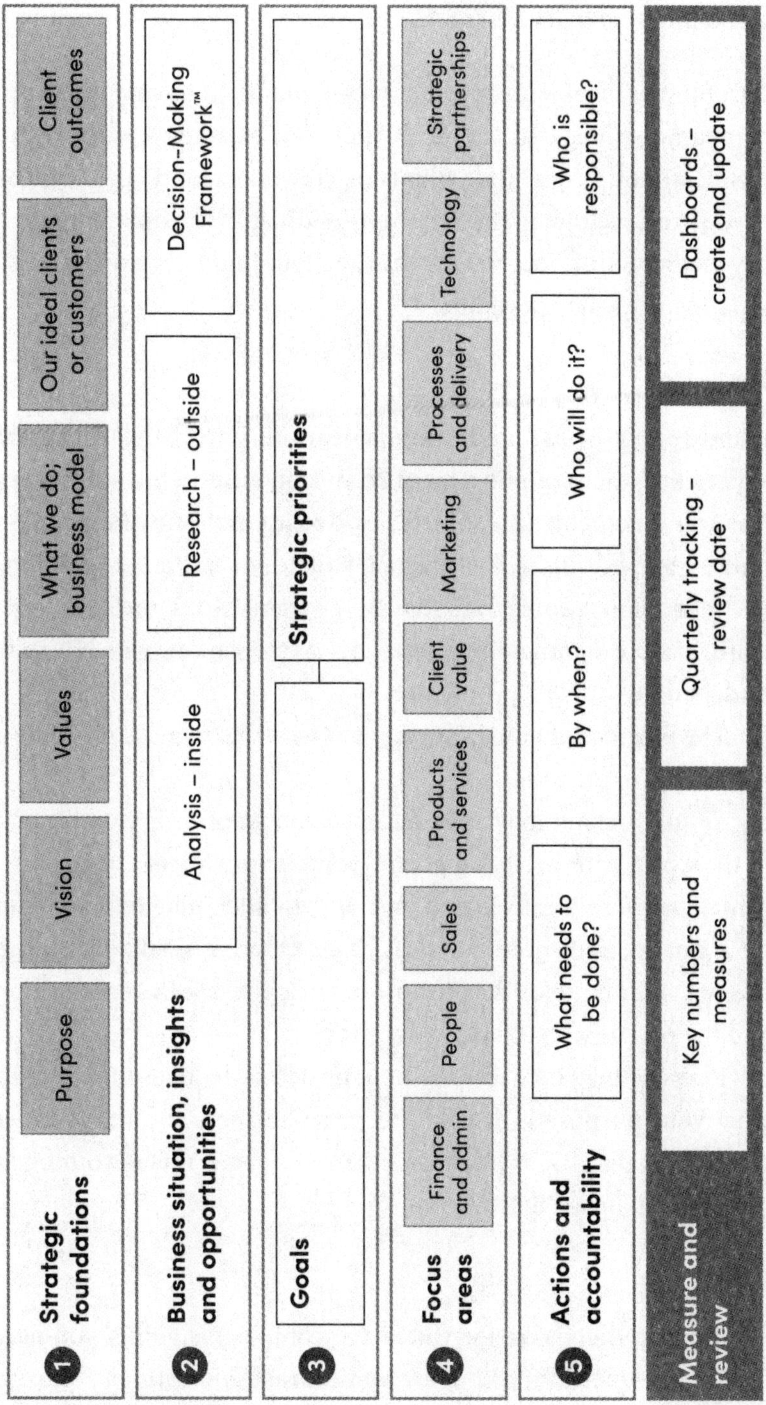

Strategic foundations

I group these elements together as the foundations that underpin the company's strategic direction: purpose, vision, values, what we do and business model, our ideal clients or customers, and client outcomes. If you are developing The Strategy Roadmap™ for your company with key members of your team, this section could be broken out into separate workshop sessions.

Purpose

I find that 'purpose' and 'mission' can be interchanged but, in my experience, there can be a lot of confusion around the word 'mission'. Mission statements can sometimes confuse not only the people who create them but those customers trying to understand the difference, and not many people can remember them. So, I prefer to use the word 'purpose' rather than 'mission' as it is more widely used and understood.

The purpose of your company answers the 'why', as in, 'Why does it exist?'

Your company may exist because you want to have a big impact in the world with what you do and leave a positive legacy globally. Or, it may be more locally based and seek to add value to its customers on a smaller and more personal basis. Often, a small, privately held business may exist for the purpose of enriching the lives of the founder and the people who are part of the team.

Purpose may be wide-reaching or narrowly focused. If you know what your purpose is, it helps keep the business and the founder on track. Your purpose is likely to remain the same, unless your business direction changes significantly.

Vision

To arrive at the vision for where the company is going, you need to answer the question, 'What are you ultimately creating?' Your vision could be to become a $100M company in 20 years' time, or to have 10,000 customers around the world using your products.

Both 'vision' and 'purpose' provide the context and future focus of what you are creating. If both are powerful drivers for your business, they will help you persevere and stay on track if times get tough.

For example, your purpose could be to provide the best data analytics software and services to help marketing companies be more competitive. Your vision could be to become the number-one supplier of data analytics software and services in a geographic area (local or global), or to have 60% market share within five years.

If you haven't defined your vision, play around with the concept to identify something that is exciting, a stretch but possible and something to work towards.

Again, fine-tuning your company's purpose and vision could be done in a workshop session.

Values

When you have clear values for your business, decisions become easier.

There will be times when you are in unchartered waters. You have no reference points and you aren't entirely sure what to do. When you experience challenges, and even new opportunities, referring back to your values keeps the important stuff top of mind.

For example, a wonderful opportunity presents itself and all the numbers and justification stack up, but it means doing business with someone whose mode of operation isn't entirely in alignment with yours. What do you do? I always refer back to values to help me decide.

If you are conflicted about what you are thinking of doing, or a situation you are facing is challenging your decisions, keep your values front and centre to provide the direction you are seeking. Decisions may not be easy but they will always feel better when they are made in alignment with your values.

The company's values are core to its culture. For example, Virgin Unite, a philanthropic foundation to help 'create opportunities for a better world', values equality, belonging, purpose, respect and growth. These values not only drive the culture of the organisation but attract like-minded employees and partners.

What we do and business model

'What we do' is direct and clear. I also like to include 'business model' because sometimes business owners lose sight of their business model and the company's core capabilities when they get excited about big new opportunities.

I've seen boards get excited about business-to-consumer (B2C) business opportunities when the company is firmly entrenched with a business-to-business (B2B) client portfolio and a business structure to deliver to that model. This redirection can be done, of course, but the question is always whether it's the right strategy.

The hypothetical data analytics software and services company mentioned earlier can clearly define what they do and what their business model is. The business model for a consulting company could vary, but it is best to specialise so resources aren't spread too thinly and margins aren't eroded. Compare in-person (done for you) consulting services, training workshops in-house, public training workshops, one-on-one coaching, DIY downloadable programs, keynote speaking, solution implementation, SaaS delivery, facilitated strategies and retreats… and so it goes on.

As long as the company has the right strategic focus, keeping the business model front and centre helps to avoid the risk of trying to be everything for everyone. Growth requires you to be opportunistic, but the business model helps put these opportunities into the right framework.

Our ideal clients or customers

Being very clear on your ideal clients or customers will help drive growth. Most service-based startups will do anything for anyone in order to bring revenue in. However, the more specific you are about your ideal clients, the more impact your marketing will have. I have covered this in several sections of this book already as it is an important component that focuses your strategic direction.

What industries are your ideal customers in? Which segments of those industries? How big are they (revenue, employees, geographic reach)? What do they need? What are their challenges? Who are the decision-makers and influencers?

For example, my ideal clients are close to becoming or have become 'members' of The 7% Club. They want to upscale their company, they value advice and support as they want to learn and become better at what they do, they want to get there faster and more easily (less struggle) than they could on their own, and at the same time they also value lifestyle and creating a better life for themselves and the people they love. They have reached a tipping point on their growth path and have made the decision to get help now to move beyond it. They are most likely to be older millennials or younger gen Xers.

I know them. That is the point of having a clearly defined ideal customer: it helps you attract more of the same and keeps you focused on who you want to deliver your value to.

Client outcomes

The final strategic foundation, client outcomes, isn't easy to pinpoint. However, when you do, it provides clear direction for all marketing and business development activities.

The only way to really get clarity on the specific outcomes or value you deliver to your customers is to know who they are – that is, to nail the previous section. What are you helping them to achieve? What solutions are you helping them solve? What feelings does your product or service give them?

For example, a luxury European sportscar delivers all sorts of features and mechanical quality. It drives fast. It comes with many optional extras for you to customise the car – colour, interior, sports packs, sunroof, wheels and so on. It has technical specifications a mile long for the enthusiasts. But, does anyone really buy a luxury European sportscar for those features? What sells the car is how it makes you *feel*! Free, young, happy, powerful, affluent, sexy… that is the real power in the car's value proposition.

*

Once you have all these foundations in place, they will act as a compass to keep you and your team on track, and also clearly inform new employees of the strategic direction of the company.

Business situation, insights and opportunities

Good preparation provides a framework for making sound strategic decisions and removing the guesswork around which direction to take your company in.

Either this section or the section on strategic foundations can be completed first. As long as you work through both, it doesn't matter where you start.

These are the key elements of preparation that you can do yourself, delegate to your key people or work on together. Once they have been done, they could be reviewed and prioritised, and have decisions made around them, in a workshop session. Keep it simple, make it easy.

Analysis – inside the business

The starting point for strategy is analysis of what's happening *inside* your business.

When I talk about knowing what's really going on in your business, I'm referring to the key drivers that make you money and propel you forward, and those that don't. Two of the most important drives are clients, and products and services. I cannot overestimate how important these are because they are critical to strategic planning.

My number-one starting point for analysis is your **client base**. It is essential to understand your client base and which clients are the most profitable, spend the most with you, have long tenure with your company and enable you to continue delivering new products and services as they grow. Knowing who these clients are and what proportion they are of your whole client base will enable you to identify the exact type of client you want more of. It will impact your marketing message as you 'talk to' those clients rather than the ones you want less of. It will also drive your sales and channel activities as you narrow your focus to bringing in more of these ideal clients.

Equally important is the analysis of your **product and service portfolio**. You may have multiple streams of revenue from different products, services or brands. As I go through in detail in other chapters, in addition to sales revenue, what is also important is the contribution these products make to your margin. Some products deliver more to your business with less effort while others consume resources and add complexity to your business.

Analyse your product and service margins, and analyse the stock-keeping units (SKUs) associated with each product, including components and packaging. This inventory needs to be stored, picked and packed, replenished, kept track of and reported on. This costs money, requires people, systems and infrastructure and can add considerable complexity to your business if not managed well.

I did an analysis of a client's brands as preparation for a strategic retreat I was running with their team. One brand only generated 8% of the company's sales at a much lower margin than the other brands. Based on that, we could have made various decisions about sourcing, getting better cost of goods and margin, or marketing to ramp up sales volume. However, when we looked at the ratio of SKUs for that brand compared to the others, it carried 50% of the total SKUs and, as a result, required a lot of resources to manage that stock. By comparison, their top-selling brand with high sales and high margin only had 7% of SKUs.

So, understanding which products and services are your stars and which aren't is essential for future planning.

Finally, the third critical component of analysis is a **SWOT** – to do an analysis of your company's strengths, weaknesses, opportunities and threats. This analysis will form a core part of your strategy. Strengths and weaknesses are internal attributes of your business. Threats are external to your business – some examples include exchange rate variation, the threat of cheap imports, the threat of technology making your product or service redundant and bigger cash-rich competitors entering your market to dominate it. Opportunities are also external to your business and include things like growth from entering new geographic markets or customer segments, new products or licences to acquire and the acquisition of competitors.

When identifying your strengths and weaknesses, you need to be brutally honest, because strengths can be made stronger and help your business grow, and weaknesses need a strategy to help mitigate them.

Once my clients have completed a SWOT analysis, I take them through the step of matching their strengths with their opportunities and their weaknesses with their threats. This helps identify where you can capitalise most on opportunities when you are in a position of strength. It also highlights your least defendable position, where you have an inherent weakness and you are faced with a real threat – for example, a larger, cashed-up competitor is entering your market and one of your weaknesses is tight cashflow. Some of these scenarios will certainly need a strategy, but doing the analysis and knowing what you need to address is the first step.

All these factors I've been through are critical for the analysis inside your company. Analysis gives you clarity.

Research – outside the business

Research is important because, for most business owners, it is where innovation and fresh ideas come from. I find this quite a creative component of strategy. This is about looking and stepping *outside* your business.

There are many places to conduct research. I usually start with companies in the **same industry overseas**. I always find ideas and inspiration in other countries' industry leaders. I have even set up meetings with the heads of these companies if I plan on travelling to those locations. Operating on the other side of the world is not a threat to traditional, location-centric companies who clearly have no intention of setting up in your market. Fully digital, global companies need stealthier forms of research!

I advised a client of mine to do this many years ago. He took my advice, and ended up allying with a global leader and inheriting their technology, which provided a significant competitive edge.

The next kind of research I use for new ideas and inspiration is looking at **other companies in other industries**. I like to look at other business models, too, to get ideas for new ways to deliver services, package products and services, engage employees and market to customers.

When doing your research, focus on delivery methods, how other companies may be charging a premium for their product or service, the niche markets they serve, how they position and present their brands, unique service packages they offer, and sales and marketing aspects, such as their lead generation funnel. All these things will give you ideas for your own business, which may become part of your strategy.

Suppliers are another good research source. Depending on your business and how close you are with your supply chain, the key people you deal with from supply organisations will also know a lot about what's happening with your competitors and with their own client base. These insights may not be in-depth due to confidentiality but they can provide a good general indicator of what's happening in the market and, ideally, the trends in your industry.

Another major source of research, which I advocate all my clients use, is your own **client feedback**. (This is different from client-base *analysis* in the 'Analysis' section.) Conduct some research among your own clients about what would add more value for them, what other challenges you could help them solve and what you need to do better.

My absolute most preferred way to do client research is a much simplified and modified version I've created of the net promoter score. I usually have about five questions to ask, all of which need to be answered with a rating out of ten, with ten being the best. When you then ask, 'What would need to happen for you to score us as ten?', you will receive a wealth of feedback and insights from your clients.

Using my model, scores of nine or ten will come from those clients who will promote you to others; seven or eight means there is room to improve in the eyes of your clients, although they may be quite happy with your service; and six and below means they are not only likely to defect but also to not promote you to others.

Of course, asking the right questions is key, as is not putting the onus on your clients to respond to lengthy surveys. Make it brief but effective. Also, you need to drive it. If you have a service firm, face to face is best as you will learn so much from body language.

A question I always like to include is a version of this: 'On a scale of one to ten, how *relevant* are we to your growth plans over the next two to three years?' The answer will tell you whether this client will become more reliant on your products and services, or whether you are becoming less relevant to their business and need to evolve in order to retain them as a client.

You must conduct your research with the right people – people who can genuinely answer these questions from a business perspective rather than juniors, who may give you positive feedback because they like dealing with your people.

The other thing about client research is that you must test your questions with a couple of clients first, then adjust if need be. Don't risk going through this whole exercise with all your clients and getting answers that tell you little.

Conducting client research the right way is an invaluable source of real insights that will form part of your strategic plan and help drive business growth.

The final important piece of research is to **assess risk**. Every strategic decision carries with it a degree of risk. Managing risk is about managing uncertainty. This is why it is important to identify potential risks associated with any new opportunity, the likelihood of them eventuating and strategies to address should they arise. (Note: I am not referring here to general business risk assessment but to risks associated with pursuing new opportunities for growth.)

Entrepreneurs will often leap into new opportunities without fully considering and assessing the potential risks of their new venture. Because risk is about uncertainty, we can't predict the future, but we can plan for certain eventualities or specific scenarios.

Richard Branson has often been quoted as assessing risk as a core part of strategic decision-making. He always looks at the potential downside and how his company could defend it.

I like to keep it simple and list the potential risks or downsides associated with any strategies that take your business into *new* territory, such as entering a new market, adding a new business to your existing business, setting up an international office, merging with another company, acquiring a business or diversifying to develop completely new products.

In the context of strategic planning, I categorise the potential risk associated with new opportunities as 'Low', 'Medium' or 'High' risk. When there is a low likelihood of risk and a corresponding low impact, the risk consideration would be unlikely to stop you from pursuing such an opportunity. When there is a high likelihood of risk and a high impact, you would need to give that opportunity serious consideration because the *overall* risk to your business is very high.

For example, if you acquire another business, the risk could be that the biggest clients in that business defect after the acquisition. The impact would be the capital outlay if the acquisition were not successful. The corresponding impact to your business would be high. If there is considerable upside in pursuing that opportunity, you would probably develop a strategy around in-depth due diligence with the client base, terms for the incumbent owner to stay for a handover to ensure customer retention and a good relationship strategy to maintain all the key clients.

High-risk opportunities really need an in-depth look at the best-case and worst-case scenarios, and the associated financials for each.

Risk comes in many forms, but for most small and medium-sized businesses the greatest risk is financial impact, health and safety risks to people and compliance risk overall. Different levels of risk deserve different weighting and will vary between companies.

If you identify and assess potential risks associated with your company's opportunities for growth, you will be able to make well-informed decisions on your strategic priorities.

The Decision-Making Framework™

This is where it all comes together. The Decision-Making Framework™ is a sorting and prioritising tool that will ultimately enable you to prioritise strategic decisions based on the current context and level of risk. It will change how you approach strategic planning. I developed this framework to help my clients in their planning process and help them make informed strategic decisions. I use it in my businesses and for all my clients.

As long as you do the preparation – analysis, research, crunching the numbers and a thorough SWOT – your strategic priorities will reveal themselves to you. If you don't know which way to grow your company, or you can't make a decision about where to invest and which opportunities will be best to pursue, the framework will give you clarity.

It won't predict the future and it doesn't guarantee anything. What it will do is identify which priorities are best to pursue right now. It will also identify, where applicable, which opportunities are potentially very attractive as future strategies. Your action plan for those may be to develop a more detailed business case before you make a decision. (For example, you may be considering investing in new technology to reduce your development timelines, but you can't quantify the potential gains until you've done some further investigation.)

The Decision-Making Framework™ helps you sort and prioritise your opportunities against criteria such as these (and any other criteria that are important and relevant to your business):

- the risk factor (Low, Medium or High)
- the potential returns of one opportunity over another (an estimated dollar revenue or low, medium or high potential returns)
- alignment with your company's strengths
- whether it can be done with existing resources
- whether it fits your current business model
- whether it can be done with existing cash reserves.

Once you've listed all your potential strategic opportunities and assessed them all against the same criteria, the priorities for your overall strategy will become very obvious (see table 8.1 overleaf).

This tool, more than any other I use for planning, gives CEOs huge insights and clarity for making strategic decisions.

With this preparation now complete, it's time to get onto creation of your strategy.

Goals and strategic priorities

Let's touch on the strategic priorities first.

After you have completed the business situation, insights and opportunities component of The Strategy Roadmap™, it will become clear where the business needs to focus for growth. If, for example, your acquisition of new customers and clients has slowed down, then business development and marketing would be a strategic focus. If you have grown rapidly in recent times and need to automate your business processes to get operations back under control, then technology and processes would be a strategic focus. If your business is in good shape and you want to expand growth internationally, then a strategic focus may be to find appropriate partnerships that will assist this expansion into new markets.

Table 8.1: Decision-Making Framework™

Strategic opportunities	Aligns with company strengths?	Risk (Low/ Medium/ High)	Sales cycle (short/ medium/ long)	Aligns with vision?	Can do in planned period?	Can do with available funds?	Can do with existing business model?	Can do with existing people?	Potential returns ($ est. or Low/ Medium/High	Rank
1.										
2.										
3.										
4.										
5.										
6.										
7.										

Strategic priorities will change as the company upscales and addresses key challenges at each stage of growth around structure, people and strategy.

Whatever the appropriate strategic focus is for your business, it will feed into your goals. They are closely connected.

Goals need emotion in order to be galvanising. For example, a goal to 'increase sales by $500,000 next year' is neither exciting nor directional. What is the *strategy* to make that happen? Simply increasing everyone's sales budget is not the answer. Where will those sales come from and how is the business going to use its resources to make that happen?

Straightforward goals do not need a strategy and can be executed by a few actions. For example, the goal 'to move office this year to a more flexible space' can be done relatively easily and could potentially be project-managed by one person.

Bigger goals usually need some workshopping to arrive at the 'how', as in the previous sales example. Let's keep it simple and say that a goal that makes you ask, '*How* are we going to achieve that?' needs some brainstorming first, so the actions follow.

New opportunities (from the business situation, insights and opportunities section) simply become goals you want to achieve. They need to be sorted and prioritised so you can pull out goals for the following 12 months. For example, you have an opportunity to partner with a complementary business at a trade show in a new market. If that opportunity is a high priority, the goal would be something like 'exhibit at Trade Show X and generate $100,000 in leads with established med-tech companies'. That goal doesn't need a strategy, just an action plan. These opportunities are prioritised in your Decision-Making Framework™.

The strategy for the $500,000 increase in sales goal could be something simple like 'make our company an invaluable must-have service provider to our clients'. When you start brainstorming that strategy, there are all sorts of actions that will come forward. If you have done your research into the net promoter score for your clients and gained invaluable feedback, you should have some compelling ideas and actions to move forward with. These, in turn, will take you closer to the sales uplift goal you want to achieve.

Other options could be to expand your distribution channels, focus on acquiring two major new clients or collaborate with a strategic partner to help drive growth in new markets.

When there isn't an obvious path from where you are now to the end goal, the strategy will show the way. That is the part that is often missing, as most companies go from goals to action plans. Sometimes that is enough but, mostly, you will need a strategy that enables those goals to become real. The strategy is the part that may require some extra thinking, and throwing around ideas and potential solutions, so you arrive at the 'how'. Then, working out the actions and what needs to be done is simple. The important thing to know is that, when you have followed this process, you will be pursuing the right strategy at the right time for your business.

Occasionally, you may feel like throwing in a goal that will be huge if you achieve it in the next 12 months. As long as you address the priority goals in your business that need to be achieved, it is both fun and exciting to have one goal that would be a game changer if achieved. It will need to be aligned with your overall vision for the future of the company.

Focus areas

Focus areas are the functional areas in your company where you will need to implement actions to achieve the goals that have been set, such as:

- finance and admin
- people
- sales
- products and services

- client value
- marketing
- processes and delivery
- technology
- strategic partnerships.

For example, if a company has a number of goals to grow revenue, acquire more high-value clients and win more business from a major competitor, their strategic focus may be to reposition themselves in the market as a premium supplier of their product or service. The corresponding actions to achieve those goals would be heavily weighted in the focus areas of marketing, products and services, and sales. However, in order to reposition themselves, they may also need improvements in processes and delivery, technology and strategic relationships.

The purpose of this section of The Strategy Roadmap™ is to use the focus areas that are relevant to you at the time. For example, if technology is not relevant to achieving the current year's goals, then it won't be a focus area. Use whatever areas are relevant to you or add any that are specific to your plans. If you have recently repackaged your products and services in terms of offers, pricing or fit for your target market, then there is no need to have products and services as a focus area – instead, marketing and selling your offers may be the main focus for the next 12-month period.

If you have a sizeable client portfolio that has a lot of potential growth, one of your focus areas would be client value. Growing client value with new product and service offerings that reflect what your customers want and value is a good strategy. The way to grow client value is to become essential to a client's business rather than a nice-to-have. Strong relationships and client research will help identify how your company can do that. You need to focus on delivering value to grow value.

Technology and processes and delivery often go together. If you have completed The Gating Process™ from chapter 6, you will have identified any areas of your core processes that need improvement. Technology – whether it be in the form of software, apps or devices – can help drive improvements in processes and would therefore be a focus area. CEOs who are serious about growth all look to technology to enable their companies to upscale.

Finance and admin is an outcome as well its own action area. Key actions would focus on helping improve financial strength, such as with supply chain cost reductions, cashflow improvements, access to funding and balance sheet improvements.

Finally, don't forget strategic relationships: they can provide massive amounts of leverage in the growth of your company. I would suggest that this should be a focus area of your strategy every year.

Action plan and accountability

Flowing on from the focus areas, under each you need to list the actions you identified (what needs to be done), when they need to be done, who will be doing the actions, who is ultimately responsible for them and a measure of how they will be assessed.

Some actions won't have a measure: they are either completed or they aren't. Others need measures to track, such as leads, new clients, sales by product or service, stock-on-hand levels, reduction in tech support calls or the number of workshops run each month. Refer to the section on profit in chapter 6 for examples of measurement criteria.

Planning and analysis of results and progress is essential to give you some control over growth and making it happen in a manageable way. When there is a focus on key growth drivers and numbers, upscaling will be more profitable than if growth is left unchecked.

The Strategy Roadmap™

The first page of The Strategy Roadmap™ is the high-level summary. The pages that follow are the actions and accountabilities for all of the focus areas.

Figure 8.2 (overleaf) shows an example of what it looks like.

This summary provides an overview of the company's strategy at a glance to keep everyone on track. Figure 8.2 shows an example for a specialist HR company. As you can see, it follows the same format as the process steps once you add the action items in table 8.2 (overleaf).

The detailed actions and accountabilities pages provide a running schedule of priorities that effectively provide a high-level weekly overview for everyone in the business. Leaders can keep their teams on track with the plan, and the CEO can keep the company on track, using this roadmap. These pages need to be updated as progress is made. Table 8.2 lists examples of the actions and accountabilities that would follow from the client value area in the plan.

Measure and review

Back when I was in corporate – in another lifetime and another century – we did these massive five-year plans with so much detail based on assumptions and projections that were almost impossible to make. The world was very different then and the rate of change was so much slower than it is now.

However, what we did that is still absolutely essential is review plans. We did annual reviews and made adjustments to the five-year plan every 12 months. By doing that, amazingly, we did achieve many of the big-picture goals that were set for the company in Australia. Now, I recommend doing a review every quarter and an updated plan every 12 months.

If something isn't quite working out the way you had planned it, it is better to make the necessary adjustments to your strategy sooner rather than later. This may even mean pulling out of a plan because circumstances have changed – be it the local economy, an international market, a major competitor, disruptive technology or any one of a number of other reasons.

Depending on the size of your business and your plans, you may hold your reviews as a meeting, a workshop or an offsite retreat.

Figure 8.2: The Strategy Roadmap™ summary

Purpose
Through the work we do for our clients, help support them in the prevention of diseases.

Vision
To be the industry leader within our chosen markets globally.

Values
Always put the customers' needs first.
Strive to always improve.
Respect each other.
Integrity – commit and deliver.

What we do; business model
We provide full HR services to medical research companies in a B2B service delivery model.

Our ideal clients or customers
Medical research and related organisations.
100+ staff.
Leaders in their field of research.

Client outcomes
A seamless supply of the right people with a technical and cultural fit and corresponding HR support with minimal interruption to their core research work.

Goals
- Acquire four new major Tier 1 clients who we haven't worked with before
- Grow revenue to $7.5M
- Increase margins to 35%
- Grow revenue of existing Tier 1 and 2 clients by 30%
- Win a Best Employer award

Strategic priorities
- High level of customer satisfaction
- Ongoing development of value-add service offerings
- World-class standards in service delivery
- Client retention and growth

Focus areas

Finance and admin
Implement new dashboard using KPIs to drive business improvement.
All customers to be profitable.
All pricing and fees to be in line with value we deliver.

People
Culture benchmarking.
Review capabilities and gaps.
Revisit EVP performance from last year and set improvement targets for the year.

Sales
Identify target organisations for new business acquisition.
Implement sales metrics to track and support new business acquisition.
Reassess training requirements.

Products and services
Complete new Culture App by August.
Scope out new high-level full-service offering.

Client value
Customer satisfaction improvement in 12 months.
Develop strategies to grow Tier 1 and 2 clients by 30%.
Develop initiatives to deliver more value to existing clients.

Marketing
Secure a keynote address at industry conference in February.
Develop content plan around new products and services.
Create high-value events for clients.

Processes and delivery
Measure actual delivery against service agreement deliverables.
Review processes with targets to improve.
Tighten client onboarding process.

Technology
Implement a new CRM system to support more efficient sales and account management.

Strategic partnerships
Strengthen key relationships with leading university faculties.
Build board-level relationships with all major clients.
Form alliance with our UK equivalent.

Table 8.2: Actions and accountabilities

Focus area	What	By when	Who will do it	Who is responsible	Measure
Customer satisfaction rating improvement in 12 months	Create and test questions for NPS research	7 July	Marketing Manager	Marketing Manager	Baseline scores - >8
Customer satisfaction rating improvement in 12 months	Implement NPS research program with all major clients	15 July	Account Managers	Sales Manager	Baseline scores - >8
Develop strategies to grow Tier 1 & 2 clients by 30% in 12 months	Create strategic account plans for all Tier 1 and 2 clients.	15 August	Account Managers	Sales Manager	Account plans presented to Sales & Marketing and signed off
Develop strategic initiatives to deliver more value to existing clients	Arrange one-on-one workshops with clients to debrief on NPS research and present new value service options	16 August	Account Managers	Account Managers	Initiatives approved by clients; planned uplift of 30% for year

You will need to review the progress of key numbers and other measures against all the action items that came out of your strategy roadmap.

It is important to set review dates so everyone is looking to the future at what needs to be achieved when. As progress and achievements are made, it is also important to update dashboards with key measures. By this stage, if you don't have a dashboard for your business, it is essential that you create one (see chapter 6).

The simplest way to do a review is to refer to the list of actions that came out of your strategy for each key area of your business or each major project. For example, you may have a list of marketing activities that you will be implementing for lead generation, conversion and client acquisition over the next 12 months. That is easy to track, measure and review.

A strategic plan is not a 'set and forget' exercise and the review process is essential. Here are ten key benefits :

1. It keeps your team focused on the contribution they have to make to the company strategy.
2. It keeps you focused on the strategic direction of the business.
3. You can celebrate wins along the way as milestones are achieved, which infuses more energy and enthusiasm into the bigger picture and the team.
4. Regular reviews enable you to course-correct as required to address obstacles that arise.
5. If a major obstacle arises or something significant occurs that wasn't considered at the time, you can decide whether to continue or pull out before it has a negative impact on your business.
6. Regular reviews pull your thinking out of the day-to-day detail and shift your focus back onto the bigger picture.
7. A review keeps you very focused on measurements that determine what 'success' and 'progress' look like.

8. Strategy isn't something you can 'set and forget' – a review keeps it fluid and dynamic.
9. Reviews with your key team members are a positive way to involve them in the bigger picture of the business overall and not just their area of responsibility.
10. When your team becomes used to this process, they should be able to run a review without you having to drive it. The review process builds capability among your team.

When growth needs additional funds

Growth cannot always be funded from the company's available funds. Sometimes, founders need to look outside of their company when an additional cash injection is required to fuel the pursuit and acquisition of strategic goals.

As stated earlier, I am not a financial expert. However, based on my own experiences and those of my clients, here are some of the most common sources of additional funding for established businesses (as opposed to startups seeking venture capital or other early investors). If you are considering additional funding for expansion, please seek expert financial advice on all your options as one of the following may not be the best fit for you and your business.

Financial institutions / business owner

A bank that specialises in business lending is an obvious option. It may or may not be one of the larger banks and it may not be your current business bank. Remember, you can take your business banking to another bank, as well as other accounts such as superannuation, personal bank accounts and other investment accounts; this mix is often an attractive incentive for a different bank to take you on board as a new client.

Depending on the size of your business turnover and amount of funding required, you may secure funding in several ways, including a straight business loan, a draw-down facility on your mortgage (not necessarily the best practice but a common option) or a line of credit on your business account. Your business will need to have a proven track record and justifiable projections of future anticipated growth to support your loan application. It will also need a demonstrated ability to repay the loan with interest and fees throughout the term.

It is extremely important to do your research and find the best bank for your funding requirements. Make sure you are fully aware of the impact of the loan terms and the nature of interest charges and increases over time. These bank fees and charges must be factored into your cashflow forecasting on a monthly basis once the funds have been secured. Not all banks are the same and, although they do have similar products and fees, service levels and willingness to lend to small businesses will vary significantly. Choosing a bank with products to fund small business growth is essential.

Business partners

It is always flattering when someone wants to become a strategic partner and invest in your business. However, flattery is not a good reason to consider this type of funding. There has to be a strategic fit. As with any funding exercise, a sound strategic roadmap is required so there is no confusion as to the use of additional funds and the strategic direction for the company's growth.

Business partners who already know each other well, have done business consistently together for several years and share each other's vision and values for the business (essential) could be a great strategic fit.

A business partner could be one person who buys into your business as a shareholder in exchange for their injection of funds. If your shareholding is equal to theirs as a result of this exchange, you have effectively sold half your business to your new partner.

If the business partner is a company who provides the resources you need for continued growth (such as technology, people, sales channels or development capabilities) rather than the funds for you to go and acquire them, this is effectively a merger.

For both options, obviously no repayment of funds would be required. However, these options are the business equivalent of getting married; don't pursue them lightly.

It is also critical to have a tight shareholder agreement that sets out clear steps and options in the event that the shareholders have a falling out. Unless you specifically set out to have a business partner as part of your plan after your business is well established, I would relegate this option toward the bottom of the list unless the advantages far outweigh any risks or potential disadvantages.

Private investors

Sources of investor funding include venture capitalists and what I would refer to as 'professional' investors. This funding usually happens at startup. In the example of Tar Barrel, the initial funding to establish the business came from 20 personal investors who all shared the vision for the company.

In an established business, if you are able to demonstrate a real opportunity for growth and a return to the investor, you may be able to find someone to back your company's expansion plan in exchange for equity. This kind of investor could also be referred to as an angel investor. They are usually high-net-worth individuals who will still want a return on their investment at some exit point.

If you were to go down this path, you would need to consider what the exit strategy may be. It could require you to sell your business in the future to repay their investment, or to release the private investor via a change in shareholders with a vehicle like an initial public offer (IPO) or acquisition.

As with any equity shareholder, an angel investor may want to be involved in helping your business grow and succeed. This could be a highly advantageous to the business, or it could be disruptive to the business owner, depending on the personalities and motivations of the people involved. What that involvement looks like would also need to be made clear at the outset.

Again, it is common for repayments to be made at the conclusion of this relationship when the investor exists the business. Obviously, the funds repaid are commensurate with their equity value and pre-agreed terms.

Value drivers

Now that we've talked about how to develop a strategy to upscale, let's touch on the endgame. If you think you might sell your business in the future or want to bring in investors, growing valuable assets will be important.

Assets can be tangible, including real estate (buildings, warehouses, land), stock and raw materials, plant and equipment, office furniture and computers. Intangible assets include intellectual property assets such as customer databases, methodologies, software, marketing systems, designs, patents, trademarks and copyright, as well as goodwill and brand recognition.

It is worth noting that, typically, 75% of a company's assets are intangible. (For more specific information on asset valuation you will need to consult financial and legal experts in this area.)

Valuations can be based on the market value of a tangible asset – for example, the market rate for a particular type of building in a specific area. The value of these assets is driven up if someone values what you have more highly than anyone else and will pay a premium to acquire it; it is just like buying or selling real estate. Intangible assets are more difficult to estimate because they don't necessarily have a comparable market value as such.

I always urge my product-based clients to develop a brand. I know it takes development time and testing, funds are required upfront to finance production and lots of targeted and consistent marketing is needed to gain traction. However, acquirers will pay for brands over more generic products. Brands that are years old and have languished over time are sought after by companies looking to breathe new marketing life into them and build them up as valuable assets again.

When a business is sold, the total asset valuation (assets less liabilities) is taken into account, along with other considerations such as the future earning potential of the business for the acquirer (or investor).

As a very rough guide, a multiple of three times earnings (profit) is how many business owners start with a possible valuation of their business. There are many ways to value a business and this is included more as a conceptual guide than a specific framework. For example, in this scenario, a business with a profit of $1.8 million could have a valuation of three times that, which would be $5.4 million. The asset valuation is factored into the final figure. A business founder may have a goal of selling for $1 million, so they would need to be making in the vicinity of $300K to $350K in profit.

There are industries that pay multiples way higher than this. Big multiples are based on expectations of future earnings multiplying once the acquired business is rolled into something larger with resources that enable scaling up much faster. The scale and the terms of the acquisition vary considerably depending on the type of business, the industry and the future potential as seen by investors and acquirers. It also depends on the acquiring company and its funding capabilities. Multiples can vary from three to fifteen as an indicative range.

After this chapter we profile Fillr and one of its founders, Chad Stephens. Their first startup, 1Form, was sold for a multiple of six times earnings because of the potential future value for the acquiring company.

On a smaller scale, if a founder sold their business for a multiple of three, for example, let's look at how that is impacted by different profit and revenue levels. 'Profit' used in valuations is typically earnings before interest tax depreciation and amortisation (EBITDA), which basically puts comparisons of profit on the same level for businesses, excluding these other factors. Here are some comparisons:

- 8% EBITDA on business doing \$2M in sales with a multiple of 3: (.08 × 2,000,000) × 3 = \$480,000
- 10% EBITDA on a business doing \$3M in sales with a multiple of 3: (0.1 × 3,000,000) × 3 = \$900,000
- 10% EBITDA on business doing \$5M in sales with a multiple of 3: (0.1 × 5,000,000) × 3 = \$1,500,000
- 12% EBITDA on business doing \$10M in sales with a multiple of 3: (0.12 × 10,000,000) × 3 = \$3,600,000

This calculation guideline provides some extremely rough examples of possible 'multiple' valuation scenarios. I have included them for those who may be considering a sale in the future to show how increases in sales revenue and profit (and, of course, the multiple) can make a big difference to results. If you do plan on selling, keep this in mind during your strategic planning process.

Upscaling

Case Study: Gush Global

Andrew Fox, Managing Director of Gush Global, was a client of mine back in the early days (for both his business and mine) when I helped him upscale from seven figures to eight. He has multiplied the size of his company many times since then and, like most entrepreneurs, has done it with hard work, dedication and commitment to his vision.

Gush Global designs, manufactures, installs and maintains interactive, hi-tech point-of-sale retail displays for global consumer electronics companies. The company has entrenched relationships with its customers and retailers over many years of working together. It is leveraging these relationships to move into the US and European markets with its clients and build a strong base for continued future expansion.

When I advised Andrew early on, his key challenge was to put in place the right team, structure and strategy for the business to support the next stage of growth. He had recently bought out his business partner and was on a mission to grow. He basically needed to 'reset' the business.

Fast-forward to today and his group of retail experience companies is indeed global, with multiple locations in China, Hong Kong, Australia and New Zealand and with ambitions for offices in the US and Europe. It has taken many years cycling though periods of growth and consolidation to reach the point that Gush is at now.

His story is fascinating.

Getting to know China

When Andrew set up his first China office, he was there every fortnight, catching the midnight flight from Melbourne to Hong Kong. As soon as he landed, he headed straight to the factories. He did this consistently for 12 months. As he explains it, he networked in the western pubs in Dongguan and got to know the expats on the ground, and eventually employed some people he met there. He learnt all the tricks of doing business in China by being present and building trusted relationships with friends and factories. He moved his supply chain away from the westernised areas of China to the domestic Chinese manufacturing provinces. By doing this, he reduced costs and his products were not being seen in factories by his local competitors back home. He thought if he could conquer China, he could conquer anywhere.

This persistence and commitment to really understand the market he was playing in, and partnering with local companies to manufacture leading-edge designs, gave Gush a huge market advantage. It understood the nuance of working in China. It was able to lower its cost base by moving into the more distant manufacturing provinces, and Andrew was able to build a local network that would result in new resources for the team and invaluable market insights.

A major turning point

It was around this time that he realised again he didn't have the right people on the bus, and he didn't have a laser focus on wanting to conquer one thing.

A pivotal point was when he stopped trying to 'be everything to everyone' and looked at the most profitable and high-demand niche for his business to concentrate on. Gush already had a strong foothold in the consumer electronics niche, where innovation and new product development are constant, and that is where Andrew decided to concentrate. He has key people on his team who have strong relationships with their customers and industry players. As Andrew says, with a laser focus and staying true to the vision of market domination, everything started to move in that direction. Design, technology, installations and manufacturing locally and offshore – he put all the pieces of the puzzle together and now Gush dominates its market niche.

250% growth in five years

Andrew's business grew from low seven figures to eight figures within the first ten years. In the last five years (at the time of writing) it has grown 250%.

A huge strategic shift happened in the business five years ago. Andrew employed a trusted friend to head up the businesses in China – someone he had known for many years who was working in Shanghai in a technology company. They met in the pub (seems to be an important location in the Gush story!) and they wrote the business plan on the back of a serviette. Tim said, 'The vision moving forward is that we're going to be a technology company'. They hashed out the big-picture strategy and milestones for the next five years of growth. This is now framed and sits in Andrew's office. They then started putting in place the pieces for this big vision.

Back in Australia, Andrew was busy building his team and crucial to its success was employing a general manager to run the day-to-day operations of Gush Global. As a people person, Phil was brought in and tasked with finding the best people and changing the culture. With the right people on the bus, Gush is hurtling toward the achievement of the big vision. Having three top heads of the businesses working in sync has enabled the company's expansion and allowed it to flourish through the COVID-19 years.

The Gush team has stepped up and they all feel like they're part of creating something big. Andrew's dream was always to create opportunities for growth of his employees. The expansion into overseas markets now allows his dream to come alive by enabling staff to move internationally. His key staff all have focus and are enabled to make decisions and do what they are there to do.

In addition to an A-Team, supporting the growth plans for this global operation is a huge focus on processes. Gush uses technology to run its processes and has built a scalable system, which it is constantly refining. The system was built to be fully integrated with all businesses in the group.

Good people, robust processes, enabling technology, a strong client base and visionary plans – that's the company and the team.

What about the leader?

Shifts as the leader

As any business grows, the owner must step away and let the team get on with running the company day-to-day. It's interesting to watch the evolution of the owner into CEO and leader as the team evolves in capability. Leading a sizeable eight-figure company is very different from the CEO's early role running a low-seven-figure business. Leaders embrace their change in role differently and have varied versions of 'letting go' and 'leading'.

It's a bit of a chicken and egg argument: which comes first, the capable team or the evolved CEO? The truth is that they enable each other.

Gush has more transparency within the team than ever before as they are all senior people. The gap between the leader and the next level has reduced as the company has grown and brought in the talent it needs to achieve its big goals.

Andrew's team has opened its thinking to opportunities and how the business makes money, and its role in that process. He talks to his team members about acting like shareholders and what they would expect to get as a return on investment (ROI). It has shifted their thinking.

Integrity is important in life and in business. Fifteen years ago, the company had a large bad debt that put the business under enormous financial strain. Andrew committed to pay out all creditors 100 cents in the dollar of real expenses to his suppliers, and he did. Some of his creditors were sole operators and small businesses, and he didn't want to hurt or impact any of them. Andrew realised his reputation was worth more than money.

When you behave with integrity, you can sleep better at night. Overcoming tough challenges strengthens your resilience and resolve. It's a nightmare at the time but a good lesson.

Another big shift, in addition to transparency, is the trust Andrew has in his team day-to-day. He has more focus on strategy and the big picture of optimising value. By freeing up his time, Andrew can now focus his attention on mentoring his key managers and making them better decision-makers. Allowing them to grow forges stronger bonds within the team. 'Once you have the right people on the bus and you can impart your knowledge of 30 years to them,' he says, 'magic happens.'

There are opportunities for every person in the team to succeed and they are all treated as part of a big family. But, in exchange for this opportunity and trust, as Andrew says, 'I'll be brutal if anyone does the wrong thing'. This is not an uncommon sentiment from business owners because, when someone does do the wrong thing, it is like a betrayal and the pain is deep.

Leap of faith

It is a huge leap of faith in any business to pay your key people more than you pay yourself because you see it as an investment rather than an expense. You know they will produce a return on that investment that contributes significantly to the company's growth. Andrew took that leap of faith with his key people and, as a result of investing in them, he is now able to pay himself several times what he used to.

Talented and capable people are more expensive. When they deliver, as Andrew says, the ROI speaks for itself. Everything is lining up for Gush Global to deliver on its big vision over the next five years.

Business lessons

- Have a laser focus on what you want to achieve – keep your focus narrow and tight.

- Invest in the best people.
- Keep your cost base down.
- Be creative and do more than your competitors.
- Build relationships.
- Never let one client be more than 10% of total sales – bring new clients into the mix and grow other clients.
- Know that you can achieve far more with the right people than on your own.
- Have a clear vision and know where you are taking the company, and have a solid plan to get there.

gushglobal.com
soundwedge.tech
powerfuldisplays.com
retailmaintenancegroup.com

Case Study: Fillr

Chad Stephens, along with his business partner Chris Koch, is co-founder of Fillr, a tech startup operating out of Melbourne, Australia, working with global buy-now-pay-later payment apps like Afterpay. Fillr is an autofill app that helps increase conversion rates on sales from mobile stores anywhere.

I first met Chad many years ago when he and Chris were working on their tech startup business 1Form. Tired of filling in the same details with every real estate agent when looking for rental properties, he and Chris saw a real gap in the market to standardise this process across the industry. They worked tirelessly to get 1Form off the ground, starting in their home state of Victoria and then expanding across other states of Australia to cover 90% of the market.

After eight years in operation, they sold 1Form to REA Group for AU$15 million. The Fillr technology is not such a big leap from their initial 1Form app but it is way bigger in terms of scope, opportunity and potential returns.

Bigger thinking

I started my discussion with Chad by asking about the different challenges of a $2M business versus a $10M business. Chad's response was that you have to think bigger to grow from $1M in revenue to $2M – bigger than you did to get to $1M. And then, to grow from $2M to $10M, 'You have to think bigger again'.

This 'bigger thinking' requires a look into the future (as such) at what a $10M company might look like. What sort of team would you need for a $10M company? For example, says Chad, up to $2M in revenue you need about three to five generalists and they have to cover lots of jobs, whereas a $10M company needs skilled people and structure. It needs more management, which equates to more cost and less profit, and more human resources support. A bigger company can spiral out of control more quickly without the right structure in place.

This is where many entrepreneurs stumble. They build their business up to $2M using a few key people who are across multiple areas of responsibility and there is usually limited structure, with the owner still heavily involved in the day-to-day operations of the business. That isn't sustainable as more experienced people are added to the business to manage growth, which in turn necessitates a shift in role of the business owner. If this stage isn't mastered, it will be an uphill challenge to expand beyond $2M in sales.

Chad and Chris have clearly defined roles: Chris focuses on sales and capital raising; Chad's focus is more on operations and finance. Although he doesn't have a finance background, Chad says you can't delegate finance, even if you're not the one managing and preparing the accounts. As the founder or owner of the business, it is a key responsibility to watch what is happening and understand the financials. Good advice.

Compare this to their early days in business when Chad was doing 'anything and everything' trying to save money and avoid hiring people. As Chad has testified, this approach is not sustainable if you want to grow beyond $2M in turnover.

Competing with big corporates to attract new people

When 1Form was sold, the founders looked after their existing team and brought them into Fillr. Attracting new people into the business was much more difficult. All the major tech companies had a presence in Melbourne and could pay double what Fillr was offering to attract the right people. However, Fillr's weakness, which was being small without the salary-pulling power of the big companies, became its strength.

As a small company, Fillr was able to fully engage its team in the plans and progress and make everything transparent. In the beginning, the strategy team used to meet weekly and discuss Fillr's strategy. They covered everything, including who may want to acquire it, what sectors it would target, and its product and client strategies.

They documented everything and were then able to share it with the wider team, even the bad news! This quarterly presentation received positive feedback from the team and eventually formed the basis of Fillr's pitch deck. This transparency made the team feel valued for its contribution, and the founders made it clear that there was no real hierarchy and they were all equal.

Although Fillr couldn't offer the big salaries to attract new people, it did offer a sense of belonging and being valued, and the big-name tech clients it was working with looked good on everyone's CVs. There is also an employee share option plan.

You need to know what else, apart from big salaries, makes people want to join your team, and then genuinely give that to them. This won't work for every business. If the right people aren't in place, or there is no strategic plan for the business, or the owner still hasn't learned to trust that the team can effectively contribute to ideas and plans for growth, then this level of engagement and involvement is not going to get off the ground.

Fillr not only got off the ground but has soared ahead and been sold to a large multinational company. Clearly, these business lessons (along with unwavering belief and perseverance) have been a major contributor to success for Chad and Chris.

Business lessons

- Your business needs to have a good product or service offering that delivers value.
- Concentrate on your people – have the best people, pay them what they should be paid and treat them like family coming on the journey with you.
- Find good people you trust and *let go*. Your business will be handicapped and stuck at $2M if you don't let go. Give responsibility to other people so you can scale up. The only way to take a giant leap and risks is to trust in people.

www.fillr.com

Chapter 9

Dealing with the Difficult Stuff

This chapter provides important background to my own experiences growing, managing and turning around companies. I'm sure you can relate to many of these situations, and if you can't, be assured that you will experience some of them as you grow your business!

It's precisely because I've been through these challenges myself that I feel so strongly about helping you avoid them and providing the tools that will help you address and mitigate problems in your own business.

I've made this short and sharp as I don't want to linger here!

Dealing with difficult employees

If an employee doesn't add value, let them go.

Would you have employed them in the first place if you had known then what you know about them now? No? Then let go.

Don't forget how much the difficult employees affect the good ones. As the CEO, the good ones are waiting for you to do something to make life good again for the rest of the team.

As I always say, you can't change bad culture with a bonding weekend away. Bad culture only changes when you get rid of the cause. A clean sweep makes way for the positive energy of the good people on your team.

I once inherited a senior manager who I never would have employed had the choice been mine. As the expression goes, he was like Teflon and trying to pin him down to anything proved challenging. However, the day arrived when I was able to make my move. He must have received a tip-off when I headed up to Sydney to tell him the gig was up, and he was nowhere to be found. From Sydney I was headed to Singapore and, a couple of days later, by the time I'd woken up (three hours behind Melbourne time) there was message after message from my executive assistant asking me to call urgently. The senior manager in question had departed, taking key team members from that branch office. The team left behind were in shock upon learning of the departure of their manager and the betrayal by their colleagues.

I was in Singapore, the crisis was in Sydney, we didn't have Zoom or FaceTime back then and I had a huge problem to solve. No reference points for that one!

The first thing to do was communicate. I talked to my Sydney team and listened to their perspective and concerns, and assessed the mood. I talked to the rest of the team and decided on a short-term backup plan to support Sydney. We all had a role to play – sales, technical support, customer service and account management.

Then, we put all this in place and communicated with all our major clients, making the 'event' sound less impactful and significant than it was. Being proactive was essential. Focusing inwards on your team and then externally on your clients are always the first two steps. If legal or specialist advice is needed, that should be high on the priority list as it can determine how everything else unfolds.

After the initial surprise, crisis was averted and we made it through. A restructure and some process changes became 'business as usual', and on we continued. No-one is indispensable and, finally, I was rid of a difficult employee and able to fill the gaps left by the others.

Keep moving forward! It's never as bad as you think it is.

I've seen histrionics in the office played out for the rest of the team, and behaviour of this nature is always indicative of the contribution and calibre of the person.

There has been the occasional employee over the journey who has steadfastly challenged me on every request or decision as a matter of course. The ensuing conversations and communication are exhausting. If you want to keep them on your team, then a reframing of how future requests and decisions will flow is essential as lengthy discussion over every point is not appropriate. Frameworks and boundaries are important to keep everyone moving forward.

I once had an employee threatened with a brick through their window by another person in the team. The manager was too scared to face the offender and have 'the conversation'. Unusual circumstances demand specialist advisors to help you navigate through unchartered and potentially dangerous waters. I have never been averse to bringing in specialist consultants and experts to help deal with these extenuating challenges, as the risks are too high if you get it wrong. The safety of your team, following due process and avoiding litigation are all critical.

In one of my early consultancy businesses, I let an employee go. The problem was, he wouldn't leave! He seemed to block out the conversation we'd had about his probationary period not working out and came to work the next day. So, we had to have it again, more forcefully this time. That was possibly due to my inexperience at the time, which made life difficult for myself and for the employee, too.

The wrong employees can negatively impact client relationships, sales revenue, company profitability and the morale of the rest of your team, among other things.

I've helped my clients manage challenges with difficult employees, with the worst requiring police intervention (which we had suspected and planned for). At the other end of the spectrum are clients who have just needed help with the right process to performance-manage employees on occasion.

The point is, be certain about what is and is not acceptable in your company. Be decisive. Get specialist advice when you need it. Take action. Move on.

Dealing with difficult clients

As mentioned previously, my first business was a marketing consultancy. I built a solid client base comprising IT and tech clients in one group and a range of clients from varied industries in the other.

One of my clients was someone I knew personally prior to us working together. However, he became a different person as a client – actually, he became a child who was perpetually on the edge of having a tantrum. We were doing a consultancy project on his brand positioning, including design work for his updated branding. Every time he came into the office for a meeting, he would become incredibly difficult and almost yell at us that he didn't like or agree with something. It was truly bizarre and I'd never seen this behaviour before. I remember one day questioning what he didn't like about a design so we could improve it for him. He floundered around and wouldn't answer with any specifics, then packed up his bag and huffed and puffed out of the office.

After that 'event', I had to tell him that it would probably be best if he chose to work with another marketing agency. It will always be a mystery to me why clients choose to be so difficult but then don't want to go anywhere else. Maybe they've burned too many bridges and there *is* nowhere else to go?!

From that point, I handed him over to one of my senior consultants to look after. The project was completed to the client's satisfaction, we were paid in full and on time and I chose never to work with him again. I have no idea what the tantrums were about. Maybe he had his own difficult clients and employees to deal with?

If clients are challenging your integrity or testing your team, or are just plain unpleasant to deal with, make a decision about them. Maybe you don't have to work with them; there are plenty of delightful people out there to work with. If, unfortunately, you do have to work with them because they are critical to your revenue, then you need new parameters for how you will work together. In my experience, even the most difficult and demanding of clients are able to be 'reset' after an honest and engaging conversation. (Irrational and unreasonable clients, however, tend not to engage in those conversations. Best you let them go.)

What happened in my worst-ever client meeting

While working in corporate, I was once asked by one of my sales managers to attend a meeting with our then largest client. Trying to get meetings with this client was not always easy, to say the least: I'd managed to get one meeting with the head of this division previously, but that was it. The client had made it very clear they didn't want face-to-face communication. When I questioned my well-intentioned sales manager, he always gave me explanations and reasons why the project was going well and why I didn't really need to get in there and meet with them. This didn't sit well with me, but I was being blocked by the client and by my own team, so there wasn't a lot I could do that wasn't going to rock the boat in some way.

So, I was glad that this meeting had been set up. I can't remember the exact briefing given to me by the sales manager, but what I expected from this meeting and what I actually experienced were poles apart.

I walked into an ambush.

I thought I was meeting with the client and one of their team, so there would be four of us – the two of them, and me and my colleague. Not only was there a sea of faces around the board table, they had also brought in some of my own technical team who had been seconded to their offices for this project, all without my knowledge.

So, right before a room full of the client's team and some of my own team, I was publicly flogged.

It was excruciating and humiliating. The client had a number of issues that had been compounding. Had I been able to build a relationship, I could have addressed these problems before they escalated to this point. The complaints and the meeting were intense.

I remember vividly that the department head let rip with a level of detail that I would never have been across nor expected to be across as the CEO. (The fact that I was unprepared at even a high level was something I had to address with the corporate sales manager afterwards, but that's another story…) I waited until he had fully vented and had nothing left. It was only then that I could talk.

Lesson: Always let the client vent uninterrupted.

I took it all on board. I didn't argue, justify or mitigate what had been said. I made notes and also made a commitment to review and address their issues within the week (which I did).

Lesson: Your client's perspective and what they are experiencing is all very real to them, so take it *all* on board and follow it *all* up.

After that, there was little else to say. The client was visibly calmer than when the meeting started and way more agreeable, and I suspect a little bit embarrassed about playing their hand and showing how stressed they were.

Lesson: We all have someone we are accountable to and that can be very stressful sometimes.

Just as the meeting concluded, I pulled aside my public flogger and asked if I could have a word with him. In a personal way, I apologised for not being across all the issues he had raised and totally empathised with what he was going through with his clients (it was our software that was used to deliver solutions to his clients). The fact that I hadn't been fully briefed by my sales manager was another issue, based on his well-intentioned belief that he could manage this situation on his own; but, remarkably, the department head had seen evidence of that and empathised with the position he had placed me in.

Lesson: We are all people and business is built on relationships. We need to be professional and real at the same time. Also, we need to fix problems when we say we will. Also, deep relationships with major clients are non-negotiable.

After this debacle, I was able to have regular meetings with this client and had multiple levels of my own team plugged into the account management structure. Their business continued to grow with us along with the relationship.

My worst-ever client meeting produced many lessons that can be applied in many situations to produce good outcomes.

One more note about managing difficult clients: put clear accountabilities in proposals and contractual agreements to outline the step-by-step process you and your team will take when working with the client. Also include deliverables for the *client* as part of the ongoing relationship expectations. We all know this is essential but, sometimes, in the early days of growth, it can be forgotten, so it is worth mentioning it here.

Dealing with difficult days

In my experience, the most difficult days (difficult employees and clients aside) involve sudden and nasty surprises. Of course, when your personal life brings its own challenges, that is another level of 'difficult'. Sometimes work helps you deal with the personal situation. Sometimes the personal situation overshadows everything. Sometimes you just need to take some time out to regroup and recalibrate. You have to do whatever it takes to process these situations and work out how to handle them.

I've helped my clients deal with the nasty-surprise days. I'm equipped to do that because I've had to deal with my own nasty surprises that have come crashing down like massive weights on my shoulders! With more experience, the weight lessens and your ability to deal with these difficulties improves.

Many years ago, as a first-time CEO and not a finance person, I didn't initially understand what our key indicators were that could impact the financial health or otherwise of the business. The CFO guarded the numbers like they were the crown jewels. I remember one evening, still at work at about 7 p.m., I happily thought I was ready for a 7.30 a.m. board meeting the next morning and going to present a profitable and positive result for the month. Just as I was getting ready to leave, one of the accounts team came into my office (and the fear in his eyes was justified) to tell me that we had actually made a big loss for the previous month. A six-figure loss. How this happened I had no idea, not being a finance person, and I never really understood the explanation. All I know is that my day didn't end there. I had to spend considerable time that night preparing to present a rather dreadful result the next morning, which clearly marked this as a difficult day!

Finance can be difficult for non-financial people, to say the least. However, if you have a capable and trustworthy person who is responsible for reporting on and managing the financial health of the company, you should not have any nasty surprises and you should be able to upscale your knowledge in this area by working closely with this person. That's why creating a financial dashboard is so important for your business as it grows, as the dashboard shows any red flags that need to be addressed urgently, which helps you keep your business liquid and compliant.

The best way to ward off those difficult cashflow days is to have the necessary information in advance and to not delegate finances. Someone trustworthy needs to prepare them, but the CEO must monitor and understand them. When you identify anomalies, you need to keep questioning until you get the answers and the information you need. A trusted finance person on your A-Team is invaluable as your company grows.

In business, as with anything, the first step after the shock (and probably some serious venting) is to take stock. What is happening, why has it happened, what is the impact and what are the options? What do we need to do first?

I've helped clients get through difficult days with cashflow by putting in place payment plans, setting up better processes so cashflow requirements are known (and don't come as a shock) and implementing cashflow forecasting. I've also helped them recruit better finance people.

Again, terms and conditions with suppliers are important. Don't let people in your team set up special deals or arrangements without your approval. It isn't fun taking 12 months to repay a supplier $100,000 because you weren't aware of the expense piling up. If a supplier is sending invoices to anyone other than your accounts department, it is entirely possible that those invoices sometimes don't get forwarded to the accounts department and get factored into your accounts payable, and suddenly your exposure is not $38,000 as you thought but over $100,000.

Often, difficulties with cashflow occur because of one of the following reasons:

- Not all invoices have been entered correctly into the system, so the accounts payable report is incorrect.
- You don't have the right reporting in place, so you don't really know the real cashflow position in your business.
- You're not a finance person, so you delegate but don't review, check, ask questions and compare to previous numbers.
- You don't have the right terms and conditions set up.
- You don't review the cashflow forecast frequently.

If you address these potential exposures, you will reduce your difficult cashflow days.

Dealing with difficult decisions

A final word on business difficulties: decisions about *letting go* of certain aspects of your business can be challenging.

Gather data to assess as many factors as you can. If there is an emotional attachment clouding your judgement, refer back to what the numbers and supporting data are telling you. So often, business owners fail to make these necessary decisions because they ignore the data and vote with their hearts. They are emotionally attached to decisions. 'Emotional interference' slows us down, clouds our thinking and hijacks our thoughts.

When you innately know the decision to be made but delay making it, you are compounding the pain and keeping yourself stuck. It doesn't help the business, either.

When faced with a difficult decision, I make a 'trial decision'. If that decision still feels right the next day and I haven't swayed to a different option, I know that is the decision I have made: it moves from 'trial decision' to 'actual decision'. This is an effective tool to use when you've been struggling with what to do. Once you know, act on it quickly to give it momentum.

Decisions are usually a combination of gut instinct and data analysis and will not always be 100% correct. With practice and a thorough planning process, there's every likelihood that they will be the right decisions at the right time.

The more experience you have with difficult decisions, the more equipped you will be to make them. It's part of the membership cost of The 7% Club.

Case Study: Seachange Property

Geoff Oxford, originally a local plumber, read 'mountains' of business books before deciding he was ready to launch his property business on the Mornington Peninsula in Victoria, Australia. Geoff's growing operation has several spokes, including maintenance services, renovation services, sales and rental property management. The business books paid off, but it was Geoff's approach to first establishing his presence in the Peninsula market that is an interesting marketing lesson.

Take a different path

Recognising that, as a new entrant to the real estate market, he was unable to compete with the established agents, Geoff took a different path from the rest.

He focused on a smaller, niche market to gain a foothold in the large primary market on the Peninsula. He set his sights on smaller, less expensive and less sought-after suburbs. Geoff recalls that the property locations were spectacular but generally the quality of the properties was different – fewer new builds, fewer renovations, older properties. His solution was to focus on these areas and get the best quality photographs for properties in the very best locations.

This strategy paid off and he started to grow Seachange Property. The business started doing a lot of social media on Instagram with videos to promote the areas they were selling in and showcase them in a creative and positive way. That was a major milestone in the growth of Seachange.

Geoff had a great strategy to get his business up and running, but soon the next challenge loomed: gaining market share. Being a small independent agent competing against bigger and better-known franchised models, Geoff's strategy to increase share was to increase the value they were able to offer their clients. His next move was to employ tradespeople directly to 'tidy up' properties before they went to market. This took the onus of having to find and coordinate the relevant trades away from the vendors and put it firmly on Geoff's team. This is an integral service that Seachange still provides and it differentiates Geoff's offer from the rest of the market.

The 'people challenge'

Shifting career from being a plumber to being a real estate agent meant that Geoff needed to employ people who knew the industry and understood the processes to run a real estate agency and team. As Geoff explains, 'The greatest challenges were to find people who are aligned with your values and who want to challenge themselves'. His goal was to surround himself with people who loved the business of real estate as much as he does and who want to excel at it.

He was able to employ people with the right attitude, who he describes as 'hungry but underfed salespeople from other industries'. Geoff taught them about the property market and their attitude and willingness to succeed did the rest.

Unfortunately, the first business manager he employed had the experience but not the attitude and, while familiar with the industry, was unwilling to try anything new and creative. Geoff believes this misalignment with the company's culture and values resulted in a few employee departures during this manager's tenure. Finally, the situation came to a head and this person's negative influence on the company was over.

This situation is not uncommon – letting the wrong person stay in the role and with the company for too long. The impact can be considerable, but it isn't until that person is no longer with the business that the owner realises just how negative that person's contribution and influence was. Getting the wrong people out of your business brings new energy and positivity, not just for the owner but for the whole team who had to work with that person day in and day out. Don't forget about the impact on your team!

At this point, Geoff was exhausted from pushing and driving the business forward without the right team. He needed someone to help him. This is a classic situation for a small business wanting to upscale. Often, it is only once exhaustion sets in because of a lack of the right support to run and drive the business forward that business owners finally shift into the next stage. The next stage is all about structure and the right team.

Experiencing 100% growth in two years

Geoff was fortunate enough to employ a new business manager who was experienced in the property market, who put in place processes for the business to run smoothly, as well as employment agreements and key performance indicators for the team. He is the first point of contact for the team, providing advice and support on a daily basis.

Most importantly, he has freed up Geoff to focus on what he loves and what he's good at: selling and marketing properties, and client relationships. Geoff also has the time to mentor and train his sales team, another activity he loves doing. He is still heavily involved in the recruitment process and is always looking for people whose values and attitudes align with his. It is important that his team enjoys coming to work because that also means his clients will be happy.

As Geoff says, he has a sales focus and he likes helping people. He sponsors community causes and enjoys giving back to his team, his clients and his community. He says personal contact and genuine care is the key.

Once the right team and structure were put in place, Seachange experienced 100% growth in two years.

Geoff says that small businesses tend to hold off employing people because they cost money. These businesses see people as a liability rather than an asset. I would say that, when you have your A-Team in place, you can be unstoppable.

At the time of writing, Seachange has a team of ten people and is growing. This has not only enabled the business to grow, and Geoff to focus on the selling and client activities he loves, but it also enables him to spend time with family and friends and enjoy life. As he says, he's concentrating on what he loves to do and has made it his career: 'You work on average for 40 years, so you may as well enjoy it!'

Business lessons

- It's all about the people – recruit on values and attitude and look after your people.
- Make sure you have good processes to run your business.
- Always focus on adding as much value as you can to your clients.
- Have an endgame for your business and work back from there. Have a roadmap, budgets and a plan, decide what you are going to focus on for growth and make sure it gives you joy and income.
- Always be learning. Read books. Talk to other businesspeople. Be creative.

www.seachangeproperty.com.au

Case Study: Green Olive

This case study is about innovation post-COVID-19 in hospitality.

On a crisp winter's morning on the Mornington Peninsula, I had the pleasure of meeting with Greg O'Donoghue of Green Olive at Red Hill. The Mornington Peninsula is renowned for its numerous boutique vineyards, abundant local produce and enticing sheltered beaches as well as rolling ocean surf beaches. Although it was an extremely chilly morning, the estate looked idyllic in the early sunshine and the farm shop full of beautifully packaged produce was very enticing.

Greg and Sue O'Donoghue's story of leaving corporate 20 years ago to move to the Peninsula and plant an olive grove is a wild ride! Their story is one of constant reinvention and 'having a go' at new things over the past two decades, but it was COVID-19 that was the catalyst for their most creative innovation.

With around 300 days of closure, like most hospitality businesses in Victoria through COVID-19, Green Olive at Red Hill innovated by way of technology, apps and looking at what they'd always done a bit differently. How to automate? How to reduce the need for staff (who weren't available)? How to maintain the customer experience with far fewer people on the team?

They took inspiration from Virtual Disney World to not only enhance their customer experience, but to achieve that with less staff.

Here is their story.

From café to farm

Green Olive at Red Hill Winery and Olive Grove has had lifestyle and innovation at its core since the founders, Greg and Sue Donoghue, left the corporate world behind back in 2002. They registered the business in 2001 and purchased the property in 2002, on which now stands the olive grove and vineyard. At the time they didn't have an exact vision in sight but knew their business would revolve around their passions: food, wine and travel.

They moved to Red Hill from inner Melbourne, over 100 kilometres away, with their young family. During Easter 2003 they planted an olive grove, although they didn't know then what it was going to become. In December of the same year, a lease came up on a corner shop nearby in Sorrento. Greg and Sue took it over and their first business became Green Olive Gourmet Sorrento.

Sue is a keen foodie and quickly started making jams and chutneys to sell in the café and, of course, to use in their café dishes as well. Greg's expertise in supply chain meant they were always focused on efficiencies and margin. Greg gives an example of replacing poached, fried and scrambled eggs with bacon and other sides, with bacon and egg ciabattas with handmade relish, which became extremely popular. The yacht club crew would order 30 at a time, whereas they wouldn't order 30 variations of bacon and eggs! This slight shift produced a faster, easier, less expensive and very popular product. Focusing on margin is a critical lesson that every business owner should have top of mind all the time.

Greg and Sue successfully sold the café in 2008 amid the turmoil of the GFC. As Greg said, they 'tried many things'. They turned their attention to building an online presence, creating hampers and opening pop-up stores with their local produce at major shopping centres in Melbourne. They also sold their produce through other independent stores throughout Melbourne. However, focus is the key here, and they turned their focus to more profitable activities back at their farm.

Green Olive at Red Hill morphed into a destination for farm shop tasting plates of their local produce and wines. The existing shed on the property was updated and, with a long-term view, they started planting something new every year. The focus is on sustainability, wellbeing, and indigenous food. Theirs is a '100% edible landscape', in Greg's words. Green Olive at Red Hill started winning awards in 2014 and they have been winning pretty consistently since then. As Greg says, they always have a strategy and a five-year view.

Innovation for survival

Greg and Sue were in the Maldives on a family holiday in March 2020 when COVID-19 hit. Green Olive at Red Hill was then forced to close, like so many other Victorian businesses in the hospitality sector, for around 300 days.

They had been resilient up to that point, but now their primary focus became innovation.

Prior to COVID-19 they had four chefs. Post-COVID-19 they have one chef and an apprentice. How? Food service has been streamlined. They now have tasting plates that can be quickly prepared, so there is no need to have five chefs doing extensive food preparation. This efficiency has reduced their casual staffing needs, which has proved to be an area of extreme difficulty for small businesses since COVID-19.

Green Olive at Red Hill kept busy while they were closed by engaging with followers and customers on social media. They promoted their products online with special offers, enticing recipes and photos of life on the farm. Optimised posts drove traffic to their site and online store.

Their daughter Sophie looked to Disney's Virtual Disney World as inspiration to create virtual farm experiences online. As visitors returned in person after lockdown restrictions eased, they had no staff to take guests on tours of the estate. By implementing QR codes, visitors could enjoy their own self-guided tours.

Guests also place orders for food and wine using QR codes rather than with staff. Sharing platters and wine paddles simplify food preparation and delivery, and have significantly reduced staff costs and the cost of goods as a result.

They use various apps to run their business, including OpenTable for online bookings, Deputy for rostering staff, monday.com for project and workflow management, Xero for accounts, OrderMate for point of sale and HungryHungry for customer ordering.

These innovative ideas and processes have enabled them to now host up to 500 people a day inside and out, depending on the weather. Innovation combined with technology has enabled efficiencies – which is just good business practice – and also upscaling.

Business lessons

- Customers and staff are critical for success.
- Margin needs to be top of mind in decision-making.
- Try new things; be innovative.
- Love what you do and have fun.
- Treat your people very well, like part of the family.
- Have a strategy and measure against it.
- Implement solid business management systems.
- Be adaptable in shorter-term plan periods.
- You have to be willing to take risks but smart enough to assess and manage risk.
- Resilience is essential.

www.greenolive.com.au

Conclusion

Making the Shift to 'The 7% Club'

A business may spend ten years struggling to grow from $1M to $2M and just not get there in spite of consistent effort. Another business may take ten years to grow to $10M.

The CEO who takes advice and constantly learns how to be and do better is a world away from the frantic business owner who won't seek advice, won't listen even when advice is proffered, and steadfastly refuses to let go of anything and trust someone else.

Many of my clients take around two to three years to double their turnover – in a manageable way. That is because they want to and they are willing to take advice. The 'letting go' bit usually takes a while but they all get there in the end!

Many factors at play

Why do some businesses break through $2M in sales and progress toward $10M, and others don't? There aren't any definitive explanations, but I do know there are some key considerations that determine how far they grow.

Vision of the owner

Without a vision of where the business is headed, it will be a challenge to justify the expense of investing in good people, and also to have the story that inspires them to join for the ride. It is difficult to inspire a team with a big vision if there is little evidence of the company being on the path to achieving it. As the company and the founder grow, this will come.

The paradox of growth

The paradox of growth is that, in most businesses, in order to support revenue growth, more people are required. More people add more cost, which erodes margins and profit. So, the more you grow, the less you can potentially make. That's why it's important to give so much focus to resourcing, people and analysing the numbers, as these activities will help make your business more efficient and more profitable. Forecasting resources and tracking those additional costs in alignment with key indicators (such as revenue per employee, for example) will give you the tools to manage this paradox.

The business model

Wholesale, retail, online, B2B, B2C, product supply, service delivery, subscription models for software and IP... and so the list of potential business models goes on.

If a business model changes, it can require shifts in resources and core activities. Licensing and certification can require international commercial arrangements and separate financial entities and structures. Changing from a consulting model to an agency model with a team spread across different countries requires many shifts in how the business, the clients and the team are managed.

Different business models have their own challenges. If the founder decides to diversify into another business model, or shift to a new model, it can impact growth in a negative or a positive way, depending on how that shift is managed.

The products and services

If the company's products and services aren't of the right quality and aren't competitive, or if there is limited need in the market, or something in the mix isn't working such as packaging and pricing, this will severely inhibit business growth.

Many businesses that provide a design component prior to delivery of a service (such as interior designers, landscapers or brand agencies) make the mistake of not charging enough or at all for the design upfront. They hope to win the business and then charge for the service delivery. By doing this, they are only charging for half their product and service delivery. They may find the margins in their business are not enough to support the resources they need for continued expansion.

The business owner

How driven the business owner is to grow and upscale, how much business experience they have, how willing they are to learn, how resilient they are and their risk appetite will all influence growth.

Business owners need to understand what culture is and how to build it, and know that it isn't just based on cool office spaces and fun perks. The person at the top needs to make roles and responsibilities clear, communicate effectively, let their team get on with it, and acknowledge valuable contributions and efforts when they occur. In a strong culture, people feel valued and appreciated, there is open communication, they know where they fit in the bigger picture and what they have to do, and wins are celebrated. All of that comes from the business owner and will help a business upscale.

The approach to people

Business owners who genuinely care about their people – and who provide the right structure for those people to thrive and contribute – will build better culture in their company, are more likely to have an

A-Team in place and will find it easier to attract and retain people who contribute real value to the company.

This positive approach to people must be embraced by everyone in the team as part of an enabling culture.

The structure for managing the business

Business structure includes how the team is structured around the owner, having the right number of people and not too many overheads relative to your sales and margins, clarity around roles and expectations for performance, clear and efficient core processes that everyone can follow, and dashboards for reporting key numbers and ratios for managing the business.

Commercial considerations

Commercial considerations include the right pricing, supply agreements, customer contracts, insurances, risk assessment and management, supply chain efficiencies and backup. Outsourcing functions where your business has no core competencies, if the cost-benefit analysis works in your favour, can save costs of internal resources and business owner time and involvement, and speed up the company's core processes.

The owner learning to let go

You can't grow if you don't let go. Shifting from business owner to CEO and leader is essential as your company morphs from you and a handful of people to a sizeable business with a growing team. The only way to learn and develop is to get out of your comfort zone.

In his book *CEO Secrets*, Dougal Shaw comments that founder CEOs focus more on driving sales revenue, whereas CEOs who have experience running other people's companies are more focused on structure and take a more considered and strategic approach to managing and growing a company. The latter have no problem letting go because they have complete clarity as to what their role is. The founder CEO has to work it out and will take time to actually let it happen.

In my experience, when a founder seeks external, professional advice, they will learn to let go and step up much sooner.

*

I believe that, at some point, the demands placed on the business owner from managing a growing list of factors that are all completely new to them will test how serious they are about taking their business forward. Management demands from factors such as compliance, work health and safety, employee wellbeing, investors (pitching to them, reporting to them and answering to them), employee rights and obligations, dealing with a board, dealing with risk, technology and managing debt will continue to grow. These can all be onerous for the uninitiated and can be too much for some.

Keys to upscaling successfully

Upscaling from between $1M and $2M to double or triple your turnover or significantly expand your company is not something that will happen by chance or in the natural course of growth. As this book demonstrates, there are many obstacles that stand in the way of growth to this size and, without the right strategies to overcome these obstacles, few will make it.

However, the keys to upscaling that are outlined in this book will enable you to navigate the challenges along the way and grow a successful company (see figure 10.1 overleaf).

Figure 10.1: Keys to upscaling successfully

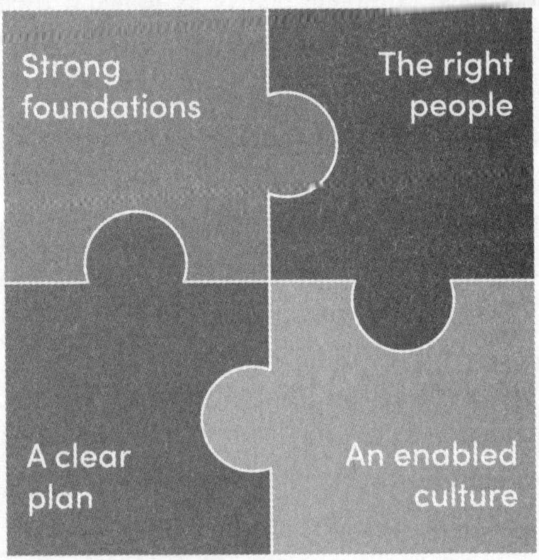

Strong foundations

Whether you wish to take your business from $1M to $2M, or $2M to 10M, or just somewhere manageable and profitable in between, it all starts with a shift.

Strong foundations are essential to give your business stability and structure so upscaling becomes possible. Without these foundations, your business will be mired in complexity and you as the CEO will feel that nothing is in your control, and it will be hard to course-correct when the destination is hazy.

The right people

In any team there are the stars, the solid performers and the occasional bad egg. The goal is to have the right people throughout your business. The bigger the business gets, the harder this becomes. However, if you have a solid process for recruiting new team members, consciously focus on having the right people in the right roles, and develop and lead to grow and maintain this team, you will create an A-Team that helps drive the business on its upscaling path. An evolved CEO and an A-Team will create a positive and transformative culture.

A clear plan

A company needs a clear game plan in order to upscale. A clear plan is visible, documented (text, images or both – whatever works best) and holds everyone accountable for contributing to the company's desired goals and results.

With alignment between people, processes and a clear strategic plan, business growth will build momentum. The Strategy Roadmap™ maps out the future and the steps to get there.

An enabled culture

This, to me, is the culmination of all of the previous elements plus that something extra. When you have the structure in your business that enables each person or team to do their job and know they are doing it the right way and adding value, and when you have the right people in the right roles and a clear strategic plan as a roadmap to lead the company, then your culture is 'enabled'.

Enabled cultures exist in evolved companies, in which the owner has made the shift to CEO and truly values their people and the importance of manageable growth for positive results. When there is the added depth of a compelling purpose and vision for everyone to be involved in and excited about, that energy propels the business and its team forward into success and fulfilment.

Companies without an enabling culture will still grow but will lack the same force of energy. I think we'd all prefer to be part of the former.

Actual results

The purpose of this book is to explore the key challenges in upscaling a business beyond low seven figures and to provide a clear path forward. The Shift Business Growth Framework™ is based on tested and proven strategies that I have used in companies I have run and that have enabled my clients to upscale.

Working with my clients to implement the Shift Business Growth Framework™, they see immediate results with growth and business performance. Clients in different industries with different business models are able to multiply their growth.

The most important consideration with their results is that these companies are able to grow in a manageable and profitable way that enables a better lifestyle. The founders are more confident and capable in running their companies and driving strategic growth, surrounded by a capable team and strong foundations. Once they make the shift, they can then replicate growth in new businesses and fresh ventures, confident they will achieve results.

If you want to join The 7% Club, the Shift Business Growth Framework™ covered in this book will give you the clarity and confidence to get there. By using the right strategies at the right time, you will be able to build a better business that enables you to create a better life.

I wish you success and happiness in your upscaling journey!

Next Steps

Congratulations on reading this far! I hope you have enjoyed this book and gained insights about your own business that you can easily implement.

Get in touch

If you would like to have a chat and learn more about how we can work together to upscale your business, please get in touch. I would love to help make your vision a reality:

LinkedIn: linkedin.com/in/JennyStilwell/
Email: jenny@jennystilwell.com.au
Website: jennystilwell.com.au/contact/

Podcast

If you would like advice on upscaling from me and the experts I interview on *The 7% Club Podcast*, listen at jennystilwell.com.au/podcast/ or tune in on iTunes or Spotify.

Strategic advice

Like the driver of a European sports car, is it time to feel the wind in your hair as your business picks up momentum, you shift into top gear and you instantly feel powerful, successful and oh so happy. You also feel a little triumphant because you *can* do this and you *are* on the right track.

Are you ready to shift gears and work with me to take your business through the Shift Business Growth Framework℠ outlined in this book? I work with my clients on a partnership basis, one-on-one, to shift their businesses into upscale mode.

Don't wait. The best is yet to come…

Acknowledgements

I want to give enormous thanks to the entrepreneurs who allowed their stories to be told in this book and have so kindly shared their experiences and advice (in alphabetical order of first names): Amy Woods from Content 10x, Andrew Fox from Gush Global, Chad Stephens from Fillr, Geoff Oxford from Seachange Property, Greg O'Donoghue from Green Olive at Red Hill, Matt Bebe from Tar Barrel, Reneé Hasseldine from Think RAPT®, Stanley Henry from The Attention Seeker, Tony Rechtman from Total Beauty Network and Vivien Gardiner from Erase Aesthetic Services Group. You have all been generous and gracious. It has been a pleasure to interview all of you.

Thank you also to my many clients, both previous and current, who have implemented these strategies to create better businesses and better lives as a result. Allowing me to work so closely with you has enabled us both to develop, grow and enjoy the process along the way.

A big thanks to Lesley Williams and Major Street Publishing for supporting the creation of my second book because now I really feel like an author! Thank you also for providing encouragement and expert advice to make the book better than I ever could have on my own.

Finally, but in absolutely no way least, thank you and a huge acknowledgement to my talented and gorgeous partner Neale. Your encouragement, support and belief mean everything! Not only have you been my major cheerleader but your creative ideas and brainstorming, patient listening and feedback have been invaluable. Plus, your wonderful, imaginative illustrations throughout the book are the real winners: they've provided personality to this book and set it apart by adding lightness and humour to chapters with charts and numbers, they are the creative antithesis to business logic, and I'm sure that readers will smile and laugh because of them, like I do. You are the most wonderful partner in the world and I love you to infinity.

About the Author

Jenny Stilwell is a strategy advisor and business mentor who gets tangible, measurable results for her clients.

She helps CEOs take control of growth as they upscale along the path from seven to eight figures by putting in place the right strategy and structure they need for continued growth. Her philosophy is that your business should be an enabler of a better life rather than something that tethers you to it. She helps her clients to take back control of their businesses and their lives, get out of overwhelm and move ahead.

Throughout her career she has had several CEO roles, including running a publicly listed company. She has also established three of her own consultancies over the last 30 years, servicing clients in a vast range of industries. This has enabled her to fully understand her clients and what they are dealing with. She has helped them solve many seemingly impossible challenges so they can move forward and grow their companies into valuable entities.

She has a double degree from the University of Melbourne, has been a finalist in the Telstra Business Women's Awards and has graduated from the Australian Institute of Company Directors.

Jenny is also the author of *Small Business CEO*, which has sold in many countries around the world.

References

Australian Small Business and Family Enterprise Ombudsman, 'Small Business Counts December 2020', report, 2020 asbfeo.gov.au/sites/default/files/2021-11/ASBFEO%20Small%20Business%20Counts%20Dec%202020%20v2_0.pdf.

Heinz, K, '42 shocking company culture statistics you need to know', Built In, 2 October 2019, builtin.com/company-culture/company-culture-statistics.

PwC, 'The Future of Work: What workers want: winning the war for talent', report, 2021 pwc.com.au/important-problems/future-of-work/what-workers-want-report.pdf.

Robinson, AS, 'What is the average small business turnover in the UK?', Business Advice, 19 October 2021, businessadvice.co.uk/finance/average-small-business-turnover/.

Small Business Trends LLC, 2021, smallbiztrends.com.

Venkataramani, S, 'Make way for a more human-centric employee value proposition', Gartner, 13 May 2021, gartner.com/smarterwithgartner/make-way-for-a-more-human-centric-employee-value-proposition.

Index

1Form 165, 173
80/20 snapshot, the 17-18

ad hoc approaches 16, 32, 105
accountability 27, 46, 51, 52, 87-88, 91-94, 97, 107, 111, 126, 137-139, 156-159, 182, 184, 203
Afterpay 173
Amazon 122
analysis of business 144-146
- client base 144-145
- product and service portfolio 145
- SWOT (strengths, weaknesses, opportunities and threats) 146, 150
Apple 122
A-Team 48, 51, 52, 62, 87-88, 107-108, 108-120, 169-169, 202-203
- aligning 119-120
- assembling 108-112, 199-200
- assimilating 112-119
- capabilities 107, 131-132, 170
- roles 66, 87-88, 109, 206
Attention Seeker, The 98-101
Australia 22-23
Australian Institute of Company Directors 66, 102
Barriers to growth 27-28, 34-36, 44, 45-51, 71
Bebe, Matt 58-62
brands, value of 13, 145, 147, 164-166
Branson, Richard 38
business model 13, 56-57, 142

capability 51, 52, 85-87, 131-132, 170
Capability Gap™, The 51, 85-87, 90, 131-132
Carman's 122
cashflow 70-71, 71, 74, 100-101, 127, 185-186
Cavelle, Jan 27-28
CEO, leadership as 107, 121-124, 125-126, 128, 170-171
CEO Lens™, The 51, 108, 120-124, 124-128
CEO Secrets (Shaw) 200-201
China 167-168, 169
clients and customers 142-143, 144, 147, 195
- difficult clients 180-184
- outcomes 143-144
Colour by TBN 133
commercial protection 36, 127

communication 5, 27, 33, 40-41, 115-116, 118-119, 121, 124, 178-179, 181-182, 199
complexity 4, 16, 30, 41, 46-50, 52, 60-61, 71, 74-76, 82, 85-86, 131, 145, 202
Content 10x 129-132
control 27, 31, 34-35, 39, 44, 45-48, 52-53, 65-67, 73, 86, 90, 95, 113, 121, 151, 156, 173, 202
creation of value 125, 126-127
culture 14-15, 57, 99-100, 103-104, 108, 110-116, 119, 124, 125, 127, 130-131, 135, 178, 199-200, 202-203
– toxic 113, 124, 178

dashboards 5, 36, 51, 62, 65, 66-79, 95-97, 120, 123-124, 127, 139, 158, 160, 185, 200
day-to-day operation management 36, 38, 47, 49-50, 52, 55-56, 56-57, 86, 100, 107, 120, 124, 125, 131, 132
'Death Valley' 27-28
Decision-Making Framework™, The 139, 150-153
decisions and decision-making 39-40, 49, 134, 150-151, 186-187
delegating 31, 32, 87-89, 91-94, 144, 185, 186
Dent Global 28
Deputy 194
Designer Brands (DB) 133
develop and lead 51, 107-128
direct reports (people) 111-112
Disney 122
'doing' (vs 'leading') 36-37, 38-39, 48-49, 85, 128

employees 47, 57, 65, 84-94
– capability 108, 131-132, 170
– core functions and roles 90-94
– feedback 114-115, 116-118
– growth and development 115
– letting people go 110
– management of 47, 48-49, 57, 59-60, 60-61, 74, 84-94, 99-100, 103-104, 112-119, 178-180
– onboarding 47, 99-100, 114
– people strategy 114-115, 199-200, 202-203,
– reality check 113
– recruitment 33-34, 36, 37, 109-112, 114, 132, 134, 134-135, 168, 169-170, 170-172, 173-175, 189-190, 191, 199-200
– retention 112-113
– revenue per employee 74-76
– right person, right role 109-110, 111, 136, 170-171
– value proposition (EVP) 108, 114-118, 134-135, 175

Employment Hero 14
Erase Aesthetic Services Group 102-105, 135

Fillr 135, 165, 173-175
flexible working 115, 118-119, 129-131, 134-135
founder-director 66, 206
Fox, Andrew 167-171

Gardiner, Vivien 102-105
Gating Process™, The 81-84, 87, 88, 155,
general manager 87-88
Hasseldine, Renée 55-58
'Get Visual' signature system 56
goals 8, 9-12, 16, 119, 132, 137, 170-172, 173-174
– and strategic priorities 151-54
– focus areas 154-156
– personal vs financial 14-15, 37
Gow, Andrew 60
Green Olive 58, 192-195
growth
– ceiling 21
– speed of 7-8
– vs scale 13-14
– with products 31-33
– with services 33-34
Gush Global 167-172

Harnish, Verne 28
Headcount 74, 76
Henry, Stanley 98-101
HungryHungry 194

INIKA Organic 133
intellectual property 55-57
investing 38, 61

Jan Marini Skin Research (JMSR) 102, 104

Kelly, Stephen 27-28
key performance indicators (KPIs) 33, 52, 79, 119-120, 127
Koch, Chris 173-175

'letting go' 48-49, 62, 86, 135, 170-171, 186-187, 197, 200-201
lifestyle 6, 14, 37, 53, 60-61, 63, 85, 143, 204,

marketing 7, 14, 67, 78-79, 83, 96-97, 139, 142-147, 151, 155, 158-159, 164-165
monday.com 194
Mornington Peninsula Brewery 58-60

O'Donoghue, Greg 192-195
O'Donoghue, Sue 192-195
OpenTable 194
operational support (and lack of) 46, 48-49, 52, 79, 120
OrderMate 194
overheads 8, 13-14, 29, 60-62, 68-70, 86, 200
Oxford, Geoff 188-191

Pareto principle, the 17
people management 47, 48-49, 57, 59-60, 60-61, 74, 84-94, 99-100, 103-104, 112-119, 178-180
pressure 10, 39-40, 50
Priestley, Daniel 28
process 65, 80-84, 99-100, 155
profit and loss reports and statements (P&L) 52, 67, 68-70, 72, 119

Raww Cosmetics 133
REA Group 173
Rechtman, Tony 133-136
recruitment
criteria 110, 111, 125, 199
relationships 36, 59, 100-101, 125, 127, 167-168, 183
remote work and teams 115, 118-119, 129-131, 134-135
reports 5, 36, 51, 62, 65, 66-79, 95-97, 120, 123-124, 127, 139, 158, 160, 185, 200
research outside of the business 146-150
resource-mapping 90-94
responsibility 5, 18, 27, 48-49, 51, 85-94, 97, 107-109, 111, 115, 120, 124-128, 139, 156, 185, 199
return on investment (ROI) 74-76, 170, 171
risk
– assessment 37-38, 127, 148-150, 152
– management 127, 195
– opportunity 61
– personal 37-38

Seachange Property 58, 188-191
selling a business 12-13, 163-166, 173-175
Share Your Passion (Hasseldine) 55
Shift Business Growth Framework™, The 44, 45-46, 49, 50-51, 51-54, 121, 203-204, 205-206
Stephens, Chad 173-175
'stepping back' (and up) 34, 56-57, 65, 120, 131-132
strategy 8, 14-15, 16, 17-18, 19, 51, 52, 52-52, 53, 60-63, 103, 105, 121-124, 124, 125, 126-127, 136, 137, 151-154, 188-189, 191, 200-201
– business 125, 126-127, 132, 190-191
– foundations 51, 123-124, 138-139, 140-144, 202
– planning 137-138, 157-161, 174-175, 205-206
Strategy Roadmap™, The 138-139, 140, 151, 155, 156-157, 158, 203

streamlining 50, 65
structure 12, 13, 14-15, 18, 27, 28, 51-52, 65-97, 90-94, 99-100, 200

Tar Barrel 58-63
technology 13-14, 103-104, 155-156, 192, 194-195
tethering 14-16, 38
Think RAPT® 55-57
tipping point 30, 34-36, 131
Total Beauty Network (TBN) 133-136
transparency 169-170, 170-171
trust 49, 52, 84, 88, 107, 120, 122, 130, 134-135, 170-171, 185, 197

United Kingdom 24
United States 25, 28

value creation 51, 126-7
values 6, 14-15, 60-61, 63, 141-142, 191
virtual model 129-131
vision 49, 59-60, 60-61, 121-122, 137, 140-141, 154, 169-170, 198

Woods, Amy 129-132

Xero 14, 194